My Exile Lifestyle

Colin Wright

Library of Congress Cataloging-In-Publication Data
My Exile Lifestyle / Colin Wright — 4th ed.
ISBN: 978-1-938793-09-7
eISBN: 978-0-9827973-1-0

1. Memoir 2. Travel 3. Business 4. Biographical 5.
Entrepreneurship

Some of my favorite words:
1. Tegucigalpa 2. Sesquipedalian 3. Onomatopoeia 4. Crisp 5.
Hijinks

Cover design by Colin Wright.

Chapter 7: International Holiday

Chapter 8: Whatever the Weather

Notes About Things

This Book

I hesitate to call this book a memoir, though that's more or less what it is. The word 'memoir' just sounds so pretentious. As if for some reason my life is wildly entertaining and everyone who hasn't written a memoir should just put the vacation slides away: we're not interested.

The truth is most stories are boring until you've had the chance to tell them a few dozen times, at which point they become tolerable, mine included. *Everyone* has interesting stories to tell, it's just a matter of boring twenty or thirty close friends to death until you've got the pacing down and the delivery sniper-sight accurate.

Let's do this: I'll call the book you're about to read a memoir for simplicity's sake, as long as we can agree that it's not a typical memoir. With few exceptions, the names of the people in the stories have been changed. In some cases time has been condensed, and in a lot of cases I jump back and forth between countries, experiences and chronology. There's an overarching storyline told through shorter vignettes.

There's also the troubling fact that memory is imperfect. What if I told you everything in this book was perfectly accurate, then you somehow (and for some reason) managed to track down one of the characters and ask them if they said a particular passage in the book, to which they might reply, "I have no idea what you're talking about"? It would be embarrassing for everyone. Especially me. And you.

Though I've gone through old emails and other documents to check my accuracy whenever possible, unfortunately (or fortunately) not all of the important stuff in my life has taken place online in an archival-ready format.

Because of this, I've had to fill in some blanks. I didn't make up any scenarios, but dialogue especially is notoriously difficult to remember. I would kill for a photographic memory, but until someone offers me that trade (I wonder who they would have me kill?), I'll have to settle for making most of the conversations up. It's generally accurate and in all cases fits the tone and content of what was said, but still. I blatantly put words in other peoples' mouths. Boom, just like that. I'm not even ashamed.

So yeah. I promise to relate things as accurately as possible while still being entertaining, and you can call this book anything you want. I'd like to recommend words like 'delightful' and 'dandy,' but if you feel the need to use 'memoir' instead, I can live with that.

Me

You may be wondering just who I am to write a book about anything, much less about myself and things I've done.

A good deal about me will come out through the stories in the following pages, but here are a few things that it may be helpful to know now.

As I write this intro, I've just turned 26-years-old.

I'm a self-taught serial entrepreneur who travels the world at the mercy of the people who read my blog. Where they vote, I go, and the ballot box opens up every four months.

I run a handful of companies from the road, and at the moment I own 54 things in the entire world.

Sometimes I go on TV. Sometimes I'm at enormous parties. Sometimes I hitchhike my way through the slummiest areas of a country. At times I eat at four-star restaurants for weeks before hiding out, hunched over my laptop for days, not speaking to or seeing anyone.

I've written four books before this one.

My Voice

The stories throughout this book take place at different times and places, and in some cases I felt it made more sense to approach the scenario from the first-person present tense, rather than the first-person past tense.

Hopefully you agree I made good choices, though there are a million ways to tell a story. I'm thinking for my next book, I'll write the whole thing from the standpoint of a third-person omnipresent narrator who speaks in the 'royal we.'

An excerpt from that future book: "...and then we partook in a delicious salad. Little did we know this simple folly would soon lead to our untimely death..."

Damn, I kind of wish I had done that for this book now.

A Brief Timeline

So that you have a general idea of time while I hop around, here's the actual order of how things happened:

I grew up in Missouri.

Then I moved to Los Angeles and ran a studio.

After that I moved to Argentina and traveled through South America.

I briefly returned to the US before moving to New Zealand.

Then there was a road-trip across the US before moving to Thailand.

I flew back to the US very briefly; flew back to Asia to give a TEDx talk in Cambodia, then back to the US again.

Last (for the purposes of this book), I moved to Iceland.

I hope that clears things up.

Chapter 1: An Introduction to Exiledom

Life is a Story

I pause, take a deep breath and start my pitch.

"Hey! My name is Colin Wright and I have kind of a unique job."

I squint away as much of the projector's light as I can, trying to make out details in the darkened room full of older-teenager and twenty-something art students sitting in desks a dozen feet away.

As I reach over to click the mouse and display the next slide in my presentation, I see the flier for my speaking engagement on the professor's desk next to my laptop. The design is centered around an image of me from over a year ago. In the image, I'm perched atop a desk much like the one I'm standing next to now, sitting crossed-legged and holding a fire-engine-red laptop. I seem to be gazing off-camera where an overturned chair is resting in the sand, as if the person sitting in it had rushed off suddenly and I had reflexively turned my head away from my work to see what had happened.

"I started out as an artist and a designer, and like you guys I went to school for my craft. I wanted to create cool graphics and illustrations and maybe build a website or two."

Now I'm at the front of a crowded assembly hall, brimming with tidy twenty-somethings, some in ties, others doing their best to stand out with stylish glasses or ironic pocket protectors. I'm elevated on a stage with no podium, and as I talk I remind myself not to walk around too much, not to gesticulate too much, not to elaborate too much.

"But then I ended up discovering business, and I realized I wasn't too bad at it. I'd like to say it's just a knack I have, but I'm inclined to believe that the same skills and tendencies that made me good at creating art and designing also allowed me to create businesses, like what you're learning to do here."

I'm acutely aware the audience is comprised entirely of MBA students, and that each and every one of them has more formal education in the art of business than I do. Their fault for inviting me to speak.

I look out across the lecture hall and thank the gods from as many religions as I can think of that I remembered to charge the battery in my remote. No room for error in this kind of crowd. Not if I want to maintain my authority on anything.

"After a few early attempts and failures, I finally had a winning model in a studio I started out in LA, after graduating from college. Studios were crashing all around me, but because I decided to focus on sustainable design, I claimed all of their old accounts when the bigwigs in charge decided to invest in long-term, eco-friendly solutions. I got lucky, but that luck stemmed from my being prepared. I was able to roll with the punches and benefit from an otherwise bad situation, which is a tactic I decided to actively hone from that point onward."

The podcaster interviewing me explains to his listeners that this is a common theme in stories told by the entrepreneurs he interviews—that preparedness is not always possible, but being capable of making the most out of a given situation is. I nod my agreement (though he can't see me) and tell him that adaptability is part of what determines whether you're lucky or unlucky, before I continue with my story.

"I started a blog called Exile Lifestyle, where I talked about entrepreneurship and branding and design, things I already knew a great deal about and could share with the world. Then I started discussing things I wanted to learn about. Things like minimalism, and long-term travel. Things like extreme lifestyle experiments. And it took off, and the success of the blog helped steel my determination to travel full-time."

I try and pace my words as I explain my transition from businessman to globetrotting vagabond to an audience of Khmer students, Western NGO-workers, and fellow speakers at the TEDx Phnom Penh event in Cambodia. I'm three kinds of sick and concerned my voice will go out or I'll start coughing uncontrollably, and that my health-related failure will be transmitted to the audience watching the event live online, as well as the people in the auditorium. But the meds I picked up earlier on from a street side, open-air pharmacy—along with the rush of adrenaline from being on stage—seem to help.

"And that's how I find myself here," I tell the man sitting across the table from me. I take a sip of my green tea and watch as he processes the information. Without a word, he raises his elaborately-engraved mug in salute, flashes an enormous grin, and pulls the drink to his lips.

"Well you are definitely doing things that wouldn't have been possible in my day," the man says, "and especially not while running a company, much less a few of them. So you have the freedom to go where you want; how do you decide where to go? And how often do you change location?"

"I move to a new country every four months, based on the votes of my readers," I tell the group of bloggers gathered around me at a Chicago bar. It's a few days before New Years Eve, and many of the people present have driven a long way to take part in the discussion.

Some of them already know my blog and my shtick, but want to hear it again in person. In the past, I've been paid for a full hour of consulting just so I'll explain my lifestyle one-on-one.

"But doesn't it get lonely sometimes?" one of the bloggers asks me.

As she speaks, I flash back to a moment almost a year before when another girl asked me the same question. The memory is crystal clear.

I had just spent the night with her, and across the table, over a croissant and coffee, she used the very same words, a questioning, slightly flirtatious look in her eye. The flirtation masked concern, and tense facial muscles coiled in preparation for my response.

"Yes," I say to the blogger in Chicago, and in my mind, to the young woman from my memory. "Sometimes it does. But it's worth the tradeoff. For the personal freedom I enjoy, for the opportunities I come across, for the people I'm able to meet, and the experiences I'm able to have." In Chicago, I smile and take a sip of my drink. A year earlier, I take the girl's hand and lightly squeeze it before picking up my bag and walking toward the bus station.

I avoid looking at the camera as I respond to an interview question from a tall blond woman across the table from me, this time in an intentionally rustic-feeling bar in Reykjavík. "Why do I lead this kind of lifestyle? Because I'm very much aware of the fact that I have exactly one life to live, and I want to fit as much into that life as possible. I know I'm not going to do that by sitting behind a desk."

Fade to a photo of me sitting amidst my 51 possessions. Take the music up a tick and wait a short moment before rolling credits.

Thank the interviewer, thank the crew, say goodbye to the staff at the bar.

Say goodbye to the other bloggers before grabbing my jacket, preparing to face the icy Chicago weather.

Tell the other speakers and event organizers I had an amazing time, and thanks for the opportunity. Head out in search of a scooter to take me back to my hotel on the other side of Phnom Penh.

Give a few clarifying answers to the podcaster before moving my cursor to the little red button to hang up the digital phone.

Improvise a whimsical bow and tell the design students thanks for their attention. Accept a shouted invitation to meet a few of them for a cup of coffee later.

Awkwardly wave goodbye to the would-be MBAs as they quietly file out of the auditorium, clutching their books to their chests and exchanging whispers.

Warmly clasp the man's hand after he pays for the tea. Assure him I'll visit his home before I leave town.

Pull my jacket back on, take a deep breath and walk out into the snowstorm that picked up during filming. There has to be a bus stop around here somewhere. I don't want to be late for the next interview.

Your Love is Dead, Long Live Your Love

When you're in it—really involved and wanting to make things work—it's hard to tell exactly when a relationship needs to end.

You know this, but being aware of it doesn't seem to help much. There's the little optimist angel sitting on your shoulder, always whispering, "Don't worry about it, things will be okay. You're both just super-busy right now, and everything will balance out and things will go back to the way they were in the beginning."

Somehow, the little angel manages to drown out the franticly shouting devil on the other shoulder, who screams opposition into your ear. "It's over! Don't you see it's time to move on? What are you trying to prove, and to whom? This can only end in tears! You can't force something to work if it's broken!"

But no one likes to think of their relationship as broken, especially when it looks so good on paper.

You're both ambitious and attractive. You're both smart and creative. When you network, you take over the room like a pair of raptors. You hold dinner parties and wine tastings.

You're everybody's favorite couple.

How can this not be perfect? It must be. You're the one with the problem. Obviously. Shit.

But then you find yourself sitting in a bakery-turned-bar in Seattle, with cold air wrapping its way around the tables and chairs from the partially closed door across the room as you sip drinks with your girlfriend. You mindlessly start to peel the label off your beer bottle with your thumbnail as she leans over and says something that brings the Lincoln Log monument you were mentally building to your relationship crashing down.

"I think I want to move to Seattle."

Jenga!

Everything falls apart in a moment as you realize there's no way *you're* moving to Seattle, and that this is tragic but also an opportunity. This is a chance for the two of you to get out clean; to stop clinging to each other for the sake of how perfect things *should* be and start acting on how things are.

Things aren't perfect. Things kind of suck. You love her, but is that enough to build a life around?

All of this goes through your mind as you take a sip from your bottle of bitter IPA with the partially peeled label, and as soon as you swallow, you lean in close to her ear so she can hear you over the din of the musicians tuning up on the small stage across the room: "I think I want to leave the country."

She pauses for a moment, as if unsure whether she heard you correctly. Or maybe she's processing what's just been said.

In those milliseconds you choke down the take-back you want to spit out, or maybe it's just bile rising in your throat after realizing you may have just broken up with the girl you love, the one you've lived with for the better part of a year. The only person you've ever seriously considered marrying.

Fuck. A member of the band starts tuning a steel guitar.

But her response is not laced with emotion, more like curiosity. She seems to have come to the same conclusion, and she's going along with the conversation.

For the next half-hour, you both share things you've been holding back from each other for over a year. Pages torn from your respective mental diaries are folded into paper airplanes and launched at each other in the form of clipped, hand-covered whispers. Dreams are transmitted with lip-to-ear closeness over the wailing, tinny sounds of the six-person latin-jazz ensemble playing its heart out to a room empty except for you, her, and your confessions. You both have dreams, and those dreams are sending you in different directions.

You end up setting a date eight months in the future, at which point you assume the two of you will be fully prepared to take the next step.

However, when you return to LA a few days later, it quickly becomes clear eight months is too long to wait, and neither of you can stand that kind of anticipation. You cut the deadline in half. Four months and counting.

Between working on projects for clients, you start up a blog and decide it will be the foundation for your new life. She tells you she wants to learn some basic graphic design and start up her own studio. Suddenly, every conversation is about the end of August, when this world will cease to exist and you'll each move on to new worlds, with new friends, new goals, new desires, and what life will be like then.

There is crying, mostly from her but that's largely because crying is not how you deal with sadness and guilt and change. But your stomach is in knots some nights, and when you wake up at 3am and look over at her, you can't help but think, "Am I fucking crazy? What am I doing?"

Then you remember the blog. And that you're finally going to be traveling. And you think about the interesting new life you've been living online. And how you won't have to depend on clients for money anymore, because you've got ideas—*big* ideas—about how to make money on the road.

Things will be exciting again, not just comfortable.

You know this because if these four months are anything, they're not comfortable. And they're just buildup to the main event.

You sell everything you own that won't fit into a carry-on bag or in your satchel. First to go, five spare computers. Then your massive collection of monitors. Bye bye desks, bye bye car. Eventually the bed leaves and you're sleeping on a mattress on the floor. You watch your life slowly dissolve around you.

You sell off the kingdom, piece by piece, and trade it for a horse that will take you anywhere.

Anywhere in the world.

The last week of August arrives, and you're waiting in your empty apartment, wine at the ready, already drinking because you know tonight is the night it will all be made official.

Four months ago at that bar in Seattle, she joked that you shouldn't just break up, you should make it into an event. If a relationship was good, why should you mourn its passing? Why not celebrate it instead?

That night the Breakup Party was born, but tonight it comes of age. You take a sip of wine and wonder if anyone will show up.

They do.

Twister is played. Snacks are consumed. A bunch of people end up making out with a bunch of other people.

You propose some obligatory toasts. You both change your online 'relationship' statuses at midnight, and your friends all cry for you because you're both being so brave and not crying.

And then it's over. With a click of the mouse and a massive group-hug, you're single again, and so is she.

You look over at the guy who came to the party primarily to ask your now-ex out and realize he might stand a chance. You look over at a cluster of girls who have been shooting glances your way from across the room and realize that you're back on the market.

Your eyes wander around the apartment, empty of stuff but full of people and activity, and realize that this—*this*—is going to be your life for the foreseeable future.

A life light on tangibles but high on experiences. You might own next to nothing, but you'll fill up the space with people and excitement. You'll be kept at arm's length while keeping others at arm's length and you'll have to figure out a way to build strong relationships despite that handicap.

Every day will be like this. Every day will be a countdown to the end.

You smile, take a sip of your drink, and wander back into the crowd.

Exile Theory

The word 'exile' traditionally refers to someone who has been barred from their country of origin, or in some rare cases someone who has simply left for whatever reason, even if they can return.

This is what originally drew me to the word. I knew I would be spending a great deal of time traveling through the project that became Exile Lifestyle, but it was also the latent reference to being removed from society that attracted me. Along with travel, I wanted to experiment with my lifestyle and a good deal of my experimentation could be considered anti-social and 'not okay' according to mainstream public opinion.

Not that I would be mugging nuns or bludgeoning baby seals or anything like that: it was another type of unacceptable that I was already starting to notice when I told people what I was going to be doing with my life.

"So I'll sell everything I can't carry with me."

"Uh huh."

"And then I'll let strangers vote on where I move every four months."

"Right."

"And along the way I'll run my businesses and projects from a laptop while doing what I can to avoid the tourist traps, and ultimately try to live like the locals."

"Okay."

"I'm hoping this will allow me to get a real sense of how people live and increase my perspective on the world, while also allowing me to have just a really good time getting into scrapes and figuring my way out of them."

"Sounds great. I'm calling a shrink."

Needless to say, not everyone was thrilled about my decision.

The people who really mattered in my life *were* supportive, of course, which is part of why they really matter. But numerous naysayers just couldn't fathom what I was trying to achieve, and actually seemed to take it personally. As if my doing something out of the ordinary with my life was a threat to the safety they had established in theirs.

I could understand their trepidation. I was going to exile myself and in doing so gain access to the world, while those who were doubtful or frightened of the concept would remain prisoners in their own country. Kind of a reverse-exile, really.

Over time, though, the word 'exile' has gained a broader significance for me. I've come to define a modern day exile as someone who sets themselves against established standards and aims to achieve increased perspective through new experiences and knowledge, while at the same time striving to become more capable and independent every single day. This modern day *Man of La Mancha* puts having a flexible lifestyle above all else, leaving himself open to new opportunities while aiming, bullet-like, at his goals.

Exiles, as I use the word, are also people who dismiss convention and live according to their own moral compasses. They're game-changers and tradition-makers, not game-players and tradition-adherers. They're the ones who set forth to explore new territory, carving out a trail for others to follow.

When I left Los Angeles to start traveling full-time, I wanted to build a lifestyle around these priorities. I also wanted to inspire others who might think the same way, but who couldn't quite figure out how to break free from the pre-fab existence they were living.

There's only so much one person can do, of course, but knowing the power of human catalysts, sometimes all it takes is seeing another person doing what you aspire to (or just something unconventional) to have an 'aha!' moment. A mental shift where suddenly you feel you've received permission to go your own way and live your life the way you want.

I know this to be true because that's how it worked for me. From college onward I made it a point to surround myself with inspirational people, and after so many years of letting their amazingness sink in, the writing on the wall became clear and a switch was thrown in my brain that I doubt will ever be turned off.

When it comes to straight-up value-creation, there are few better options than aiming to be a catalyst of change. In fact, just by living your life the way you want—walking the walk, as the kids say—and sharing your experiences with others, you're able to help millions of other people realize their potential without having to nudge or provoke them in any way.

That's what it means to be an exile. You live your life the way you see fit and encourage others to do the same.

Associative Mango Spray

Bussing & Dealing

I bussed tables in college before I started doing design work, or anything else, professionally.

It wasn't a long stint, about half a semester in all, I think, but it left an indelible impression.

The restaurant was called Jamaica Grill, and it was the kind of place with amazing chefs who prepared amazing food, and a staff that also dealt amazing weed. The latter was served out the back door. I'll leave it to your imagination which of these was the more profitable business.

The interior was tacky and the prices were middling to high. It wasn't Valentine's Day dinner fancy, but definitely second-date appropriate. There was wine on the menu, but few patrons ordered it; tropical margaritas were the bar's specialty.

For me, the whole situation was pretty cushy.

My sister had worked at the grill before me and was well-liked, so when I started I was immediately on good terms with the alpha-dog waiter, Maurice. This turned out to be a huge advantage.

Maurice was skinny, Mexican, and measured about 5′6″. He also had a major Napoleon complex, and as the most senior staff member this meant he could also be incredibly mean. When Maurice said "Jump," everyone did. When he said "Tip-out Colin the busboy, and be generous," they usually paid me double what they would otherwise, about $10 apiece instead of $5.

On nights where there were five waiters hustling around, $10 from each for clearing and wiping-down tables was sweet. But that wasn't the best part.

The best part was Earl, and his habit.

Earl was the restaurant manager, and had the look of someone who could wander onto the set of a 70′s porno without anyone realizing he was out of place until they had already shipped a few thousands DVDs.

He was a little portly, had a grey ponytail and a goatee, and tended to wear Hawaiian shirts paired with big billowy pants. He also had a penchant for smoking weed in the office. Or the walk-in freezer. Or just about anywhere else.

In fact, it was kind of an inside joke that you knew Earl was smoking with one of the cooks in the freezer when you caught a whiff of 'mango spray,' which he apparently thought would be less obvious than skunky pot-smell.

Unlike many restaurants in the Midwest, I made a few bucks per hour in addition to the tips I took home, so I was paid by Earl every time I left work. It's because of this that I came to love him and his addiction.

When I would walk back to Earl's office at the end of the night, he would be sitting at his desk, eyes a little glazed over, and I would stand there until he noticed me. In the meantime, I would watch him counting money and trying to figure out the spreadsheet he had set out in front of him through his pot haze.

Eventually he'd look up, flash me a confused expression, realize why I was there, and look down at whatever cash he had in his hands. He'd pass the wad of bills over to me and say "That's about right, isn't it?" I learned very quickly not to count or try to argue.

The first time he did this, I tried to explain to him that I should be leaving with about $20 for the day and that he was trying to give me closer to $80. But the back-talk just seemed to irritate and confuse him, so I eventually dropped the issue.

After a little while, I figured out I could make some mad cash only working Friday nights and Saturdays, which were the days the most waiters were on call and Earl was in charge of balancing the books.

A Singular Hindrance

Several months after I started working at Jamaica Grill, Winter Break was impending and the restaurant let off all but the most bare-bones of staff until school was back in session and the city where I lived and went to school had a population worth serving again.

I took the time to do something I had always intended to do at some point in my life: get mononucleosis.

I managed to get mono right as classes were starting up again, which was pretty much the last thing I expected since I wasn't seeing anyone at the time and I was living a fairly healthy lifestyle.

I had been playing competitive, intercollegiate Ultimate Frisbee and practicing or training most days, so it wasn't like I was just sitting around collecting germs. But I was bone-tired and my throat hurt, so I went in for a blood test and bam, mono.

I was told I couldn't work-out or go to practices for a few months, in case my internal organs had hardened: laying out for a disc with a brittle spleen would be ill-advised. Because I didn't have a job to go to, when school started up again I spent my days focusing on classes and walking around campus very slowly so that I wouldn't accidentally trip and rupture my precious innards.

I also took the time to improve my graphic design portfolio, which turned out to be a good investment. Just a few weeks after I had the blood test done, a position opened up at the University's Distance Learning and Instructional Technology Center (DLIT), a department that created telecourses and provided telecommunications services to our sister campus in China.

The student who was leaving the position was older and had a different graphics background than I did (more Maya than Photoshop, for the graphics software literate among you), but I submitted my portfolio anyway and after a pleasant interview snagged the job.

This resulted in two things:

First, I realized just how good I had it at Jamaica Grill, money-wise. I was suddenly making a fraction of my drug-den busboy income doing graphic design work.

Second, I realized I liked working within my profession a whole lot more than I liked working an uninspiring, unchallenging job that paid more money. This turned out to be a very important lesson, and it shaped where I expended my energy during my remaining college years, providing me with forward-momentum that I'd never experienced before.

I was driven. I had discovered a passion. It was a weird feeling.

Hoarding Paychecks

After several months at DLIT, another design position opened up, this time with the Publication Department at the University.

Although I was already at DLIT, my portfolio and interview went over well for the other position, so I decided to work for them, too. The pay wasn't any better than my first design job, but it was a completely different cast of coworkers and the projects allowed me to deal with clients one-on-one. The experience ended up being well worth it.

My college career continued like this: positions opened up (at the school newspaper, at the school's computer lab, at a local magazine) and I snatched them with reckless abandon, filling my schedule with responsibility after responsibility.

I thrived on the momentum, which was beneficial for me personally, though I knew for a fact some of my professors didn't approve of my overload of extracurricular activities (I'm talking *work* here, people, not drugs; they probably would have supported me in a drug habit, just not a work habit). Despite my mentors' disdain for my overloaded schedule, having so much going on in my life ended up being incredibly valuable.

When I finally graduated college, I took a job in LA, which turned out to be a little boring compared to the packed days I had plowed through for the previous several years. I worked hard though, and felt I was doing all I could to fill my days—more or less looking for stuff to improve in the work I did—even if it already measured up to our quality standards.

I would try to instigate little innovations, and although the owner of the business would sometimes step out of the box a bit, I felt he was mostly trying really hard to build new things out of the same old box. Look, it's a house! No, that's a box with windows drawn on it. Look! A hat! No, that's just a collapsed box folded into a hat. *Et cetera.*

I eventually realized it wasn't my job to figure out how he would run his life and his business. Still, I wondered how on earth I would be able to fill my days with productive endeavors if I was spending all my time in an office, desperately trying to stoke a few interesting things to make up for a whole lot of tragically boring and largely pointless work.

So I planted the seeds for a lifestyle of momentum and priority assertion.

I left the LA job a year after I took it to start up my own studio, intending to find better projects and not waste so much time 'working.' I wanted to spend more time building, innovating, living. Doing interesting things.

After running my own studio for about a year and enjoying the hell out of the new challenge I was finding and lessons I was learning, I took a step back and wondered how the hell I could have forgotten that oh-so important lesson I learned from Jamaica Grill for the entirety of the previous year.

It really doesn't matter what you're doing and how much money you make, so long as you enjoy it and it gives your life forward momentum. I had stopped making this a priority when I first moved to LA and worked at that other studio. As a result, I found myself enjoying life less *and* making less money than I could have made doing something I actually enjoyed.

Chase your passions and the money will come. Chase money and you'll be lucky to ever find your passions.

The Science of Storytelling

"But surely you're able to pick up travel writing gigs as you move around the world. It would be silly not to."

I pause for a moment as I take a sip of my Guinness. Not the best I've ever had. Seems like the quality of the brand is hit or miss, depending on the country it's produced in. The condensation on the the glass, though, is a pleasant contrast to the dry heat of the tiny bar's air conditioning-less climate, especially since the open window we intentionally sat next to provides barely a whispered mention of a breeze.

"I do pick up a few, but I'm really not much of a travel writer. I'm a writer who travels, but I don't think I'm very good at doing it the other way around."

"What's the difference? Why does it matter?"

"In my mind, it's the difference between telling a story and relating a series of facts. I like telling stories, and I like to think I'm pretty good at it, but most travel writing is more like copy for a brochure than anything."

"I'm not sure I see the difference."

She's testing me, I can tell that already. As a creative sociologist of sorts, she's not the kind of woman who requires kid-gloves during a conversation. I also know she enjoys verbal sparring, so I play along.

"Think of it this way, I could tell you about my time in Bangkok as a story:

"I meet the security guard's eyes and flash him a wide grin in response to the one he gives me, followed by a nod as I exit the driveway from my apartment building and turn into the tiny alleyway that connects my little patch of paradise with the smoggy, bustling access road that's always congested with traffic and hazy with petroleum fumes.

"Turning to the right, I pass an old lady laying out a small platter of treats for the spirits she wants to keep from causing trouble at her massage parlor. As I walk by I hear her chirp to my back 'Masssaaaggggee?' I turn my head, wave my hand in the universal-gesture of 'no thanks,' and continue to make my way toward the 7-11 a handful of blocks and a lifetime of experiences away.

"Or, I could tell it like this:

"The Laurel Suites are an excellent option for tourists or long-term travelers staying in Bangkok for a week up to several months. They have a lovely pool, an excellent restaurant on site and Internet that is fairly speedy and reliable (especially compared to other options in the area). The price is also right; you can snag a 1-bedroom flat with a deck for around $600/month.

"The building is located on *Soi 4*, just a short walk alongside a highway to many a culinary-impresario's favorite street foods of *Soi 6*, and it's a handful of blocks from the nearest 7-11, where, like in the US, you can stock up on everything from medicines to alcohol. A can of Leo will cost you about $2, and a big bag of Nori Seaweed-flavored Lays will set you back $3. Be careful, though, because the time of day where you're able to purchase any kind of alcohol is severely limited outside of bars and clubs.

"Of course, all writers and travel writers have different styles, but those are the broad strokes. See the difference?"

"Definitely, I understand why you would prefer to write in that first style, too. It's a lot more in line with the old-fashioned way of transmitting information from generation to generation. Oral tradition and all that."

She raises one eyebrow and emphasizes the word 'oral' as her eyes and smile invite me to make a stupid joke. I smile back, but I don't take the bait.

"Exactly! The second style definitely has a purpose: to present an array of facts and give impressions, and that makes it useful for people who want to find specifics about a place they are going. If you really want to retain information, or to *see* something without going there, though, the first is a much better option. Our brains are built to retain stories, because our brains associate facts and tie them together. That's just science."

She smiles broadly and reaches for her Guinness as she says, "To science!"

We raise our glasses and clink them as if sealing a deal, looking into each other's eyes impishly, each narrating the progression of the night in our heads, wondering what kind of stories we'll end up telling about it later.

Game Titles

Non-Square-Pixel Guitars

In the past decade or so, there's been a boom in research that both condemns and celebrates video games for what they offer society.

For example, I'm told gaming increases hand-eye coordination. So if you want to be a skilled surgeon, you may want to start mastering Bubble Bobble or (if you were born after the 80's) one of the myriad new games focusing on soldiers, guns, and explosions.

On the other hand, some studies suggest that violent games can numb impressionable minds to real world violence, which implies that by playing warrior in a consequence-free environment, kids may lack some of the associations older folks have with killing and blowing up buildings for sport (namely, that these are not good things to do).

I don't know what to think about this from a societal standpoint, but I do know what gaming did for me: it gave me a way to break out of my shell and interact with other people, while planting the seeds of leadership I would later need to step up to where I wanted to be.

My first real foray into gaming (beyond rolling billiard balls back and forth across my grandmother's pool table as a four-year-old) started with Super Mario Bros, a game that came free with any brand-new Nintendo Entertainment System purchased at the time. I remember saving pennies, nickels, dimes, and the occasional paper money left over from birthday checks in a big jar, the contents of which would someday add up to the $100 the NES was sold for.

Eventually, my spare scratch—when combined with that of the two siblings I had at the time—reached those magical three-digits, and I spent the rest of my childhood from that point on in 8-bit heaven.

Actually, that's not exactly how it happened. We had limitations on how long we could play with our new, futuristic device. This was because my parents, like pretty much all caring parents at the time, felt having their kids play outside was a good idea. It was also partially because we had only one TV, and my gaming came second to whatever was available to watch on my family's idiot box.

Any time I was pulled away for dinner or because my parents wanted to watch Full House, I would slowly wrap the controller cord around its rectangular, button-covered core before momentarily marveling over the miraculous device. How its grey, technologically sophisticated plastic shell contrasted so completely with the enormous, wood-paneled, cathode-ray-powered TV that it rested upon.

This is the future, I thought. Duck Hunt is the frickin' future. This must be what astronauts play. What aliens *wish* they had invented.

But it wasn't long before the future was the past. The money-men of the day figured out that these at-home game system thingies might be worth something. As the original bad boys of bits ColecoVision and Atari floundered, Nintendo and Sega came smashing onto the scene with the Genesis and Super Nintendo.

Suddenly there were games on the market unlike anything anyone had ever seen. You didn't just shoot square pixels at other square pixels, you had pixels that looked like things! Robots! Cars! People!

It was astonishing.

I remember playing SimCity for the first time and realizing that, although it can be very fun to shoot non-square-pixel things, it can be even more fun to *build* non-square-pixel things.

I like to think of SimCity as a gateway game for an entire generation. Here was a really novel concept (I'm sure it wasn't the first of its kind, but it was certainly the first popular game in that category) which made building cities just as satisfying as fighting or tearing things down. My thirst to influence the world was suddenly quenched through creation rather than destruction.

And so I built. And built and built.

I built so much that when a later version of the game gave me the option to summon tornadoes and Godzilla monsters to destroy my city, my digi-citizens would build the thing right back up and put out all the fires. As the pixel-dust settled, I fancied I could hear my citizens merrily singing *Kumbaya* while playing little 16-bit songs on their non-square-pixel guitars. I was a happy digi-god.

My creations were creating.

Moving Toward the Center

When I was in third grade, a lot changed very quickly in my non-video-game life.

My parents decided that it would be best if we moved away from the slightly chilly, sometimes warm Bay Area to the schizophrenic weather conditions of Missouri. There would be cows, my siblings and I were told, and no matter what I had heard, there would be electricity as well.

Shortly after the move I enrolled in a new school, and a few weeks later I tested into the district's gifted program. I was told this was a good thing, even though I would be sent to a building ominously called 'The Center' every Wednesday to receive a specialized education.

The Center turned out to be a fun place, not a laboratory for testing drugs on children as I had first suspected. We were able to choose what we wanted to learn from a class catalog that included everything from 'Mythology and Folktales' to 'The Basics of Programming.' One semester I was creating comic books and the next I was spewing Shakespeare.

The environment was fairly nondescript, and the building could have just as easily served as a multipurpose center for any kind of school function (teacher conferences, preschool classes, and science fairs come to mind). For all I know it did. During the day, however, we kids were made to feel like we owned the place, and the classes were aimed at getting us to think creatively and experiment.

After being placed a public school for the first time after moving to Missouri, this change-up was a revelation for me. And the teachers knew just how we little geeks worked, which made the experience really enjoyable.

Even more influential than the classes at The Center, though, was the hour set aside for lunch each day. Though I generally held my own in the classes I took, I really shined at lunch. That's when we played and traded Magic cards.

For the non-geeks in the audience, Magic: the Gathering was (and likely still is, though I haven't seen anyone playing it for a while) a 'collectible card game,' which means you would buy blister packs of 15 random cards and create a deck, which you would then use to play a game against other collectors. The trick was to optimize your deck by buying more packs, trading strategically, and winning cards from your opponents. All other things being equal, the player with the best deck would usually stomp their opposition.

Back in the day, this game was seriously popular within certain communities. For a while, even outside of the context of Magic, calling something a 'black lotus' (a reference to the most valuable card in the game) meant it was highly desirable, rare, and expensive.

I started playing because from my first day at The Center it was obvious just about everyone there played, including some of the teachers.

I thought: better get a starter deck so I can fit in, even though it will cost me $8. Until that point, all of my income was earmarked for video games. Life is full of difficult choices.

There's something incredibly addictive about a hobby that encourages collecting *and* playing, not to mention being rewarded for both with victory over your peers. Part luck, part curation. Part purchasing power, part social skills. *I can do this*, I thought. *I can learn to have social skills.*

Unfortunately, my existing 'social skills' were limited to clowning around in class and occasionally telling someone older than me about whatever book I was reading. I had a best friend named Nathan, but he was kind of riding the same social rails as I was. So although neither one of us had a clue how to deal with people, neither one of us was too concerned about it, either. We were into games and games didn't judge us.

Being good at Magic, however, required building up a strong network of friends to play and trade with. You could play regularly with the same person, but your skills and collection would stagnate, leaving you stuck in a competitive limbo.

If you had a large group of players to interact with, however, you could practice against all kind of decks and playing styles. You could trade cards you didn't need for cards that you wanted. You could increase your resources and your skill (and your skill at acquiring resources).

As a result, I started to initiate friendships with people I never would have seen value in speaking to before. I started watching for and noticing the telltale signs of card-slinging comrades from across the room. *Is that a large three-ring binder in that kid's backpack? I'll bet he's got his primo trade-bait in there. That kid with the dragon scribbled on his notebook? I'll bet he plays a straight-red deck, probably a bolt/fireballer. You can see it in his eyes.*

At that point in my life, nothing was more disappointing than saying hi to a kid with a cheap rectangular card box in his bag only to find it was full of baseball cards. *Baseball* cards? What's the point? And what year do you think it is?

Another result of my Magic card addiction was that a person's age ceased to mean as much to me as it once had.

Mere months before, I wouldn't have had much to discuss with someone ten years my senior. Post-Magic, though, I could talk strategy and industry with any age group. "Well of course you can't really pull off the Lotus-Channel-Fireball in this tournament setting because Restricted cards aren't allowed. But it *is* possible to slap someone down with a Necromancy-themed Cursed Scroll deck, and protect yourself with cycling Zombies in the meantime. It's not as elegant, but it gets the job done with speed and little resistance."

One day I realized grown men with kids and mortgages looked up to me as a player and as a collector. In fact, they would ask me for advice on how to improve their deck and their game. I found through this experience that I could be respected for my knowledge and skills regardless of my age. It was a good feeling.

And then there was the job.

Necessity & Bookstores

I got my first real job at a little independent bookstore in a strip mall on my side of town. The anchor store was

Walmart, but there was also a Goodwill, a Chinese take-out place with questionable sanitation practices, a local chain grocery store which was slowly going out of business, and Tiger Tales Bookstore & Espresso Bar. The last spot on the list became my second home.

I frequented Tiger Tales because the next-nearest purveyor of Magic card booster packs was on the other side of town. They also had a huge fantasy and science fiction section for me to peruse every time I came in, the employees were friendly, and the hot cocoa was cheap. Heaven.

So I stopped in every few days to spend the few dollars I had saved up babysitting on packs of cards, feeling secure in my investment as I walked out the door.

I became well known by the staff fairly quickly, probably as 'that kid who lingers around the sci-fi section for a bit before dropping a pile of change on the counter and asking how many packs of cards he can get for it.'

After a while, I developed friendships with some of the staff and ended up meeting the owner, Rosemary, a pleasant woman who was motherly, friendly, and welcoming, and as far as I could tell someone who was also a favorite of the frequent customers, who often came in just to visit her. Rosemary was also nice enough to say 'yes' when I asked if I could bring a few friends into the store the following Saturday to play Magic at the coffee bar.

It ended up being a smart business move on her part. After a few weeks, I started inviting more friends, and they started inviting their friends. It wasn't too long before 30-40 people were showing religiously every Saturday afternoon, intent on playing Magic and drinking cocoa until the store closed at 8pm.

Because I was the guy who started it (and because I was a pretty solid player with a huge collection of cards), anytime someone would bring along a friend, they would usher them over to me and I'd introduce them around to everyone else.

Once we peaked at about 50 people, I realized what had happened: I was in charge. This was *my* group. I did this. Huh.

Sales of Magic cards were booming. When I started coming in they were lucky to sell off a whole box, containing 32 booster packs, over the course of a few months. By the time I had my Accidental Leadership Realization (ALR), they had to keep as many as 20 extra boxes in stock, lest they risk selling out before the next batch came in a month later.

About this time, Rosemary hired me and she later told me it was on the basis of my leadership skills. While she was offering me the position, it was all I could do not to say, 'But it was an accident! I'm just one of the guys! I just wanted more people to play cards with!'

But video games had somehow led me down this path. From born-introvert in his natural environment to a fish-out-of-water: certain that I needed people, but uncertain as to how I had found myself in charge instead of just another face in the crowd.

I was also uncomfortable with the title I had accidentally taken up in the process: leader.

Unavoidable Titles

Titles help us categorize the world.

As humans, we need to understand the world around us but don't have the time or the brainpower to fully comprehend everything, so we put things into imaginary boxes and slap (sometimes completely fabricated) labels on them.

This makes us feel better, as if we've managed to solve a mystery that, in reality, we've merely categorized. No need to worry, that animal is marked 'safe.' Go back to your day.

Personally, the title 'leader' has always bothered me a bit; in part because it implies a sort of superiority, which I've never been comfortable with, and in part because the title projects an image that sets its bearer apart from the rest of the group. Suddenly, you're not one of the guys, you're the guy leading the guys. You're 'The Guy.'

I never wanted to be The Guy, and before my ALR, I fought and fought and fought to stay out of any situation that would put me in a position of power over anyone else. I always knew I was smart, but I also knew I was terrible at certain things and better at others, just like everyone else. I felt that being artificially elevated would encourage those who were not being elevated in the same way to tear me down.

I know now this isn't the absolute truth, but it certainly felt like it back then.

But I guess life at any age is an exercise in half-truths and inappropriate titles. That's why it's so important to venture beyond the thick walls of your comfort zone. The wisdom you gain along the way is usually worth the effort, even when you intentionally put yourself in a position where you're likely to fail.

09.11.2009 — Notebook Entry, Midflight, St. Louis to Miami

The clouds are beautiful.

Like really really beautiful.

I never take photos of clouds, but I took a handful. There's a second horizon formed by the loose particles that are coalescing into an ocean of pseudo-clouds, making the true clouds look like islands in a misty sea. The sun is shining in a way that makes them look very surreal, like a heavily Photoshopped background image on an optimist's desktop.

I'm on a flight from St. Louis to Miami, then I'll hop a connecting flight to Ft. Myers where my sister Katherine lives, before heading off to Argentina.

Katherine works at a fashion company that caters mainly to older people, in a state that is full of older people where she hangs out with, well, I think mainly people her age. But there aren't many of them, and they definitely aren't guys.

I'm pretty sure she's slowly going insane, but that just seems to make her more interesting each time I see her, so I guess insanity isn't always so bad.

Speaking of insanity, there are a lot of people who think that what I'm doing with my life is quite mad, and though they never say it to my face, I'm still consciously aware of this fact. I'm not sure I can totally disagree with them.

But that's the nature of insanity, I suppose: one person's crazy is another person's prophet is another person's criminal is another person's normal.

Reminding myself of this keeps me from trying to explain my choices each and every time I tell someone new what I'm doing. That and the fact that I don't really care what most people think; most people are content to live lives where they are stuck in offices 40-60 hours per week, living in perpetual indentured servitude to those who were willing to take a bit more responsibility and own businesses.

And even among those people, workaholism is the rule, not the exception, and I've tasted that drug, had that monkey on my back, and slowly I'm figuring out that I don't need to trade such a large percentage of my life for a place to live, food to eat, and the ability to meet my biological imperative (survive, pass on DNA to next generation, repeat).

So here I am, trying to put what I've learned into practice in the most dramatic way I could think of.

I've sold everything I owned except what fits into a carry-on bag and a day bag, ended a relationship of over a year and a half, told my clients I'm flying the coop, and left my somewhat cushy lifestyle in LA to move to Argentina, and to a new country every four months after that.

I might do this forever. There's no endgame decided on at this point, which is a bit disconcerting for a big picture person like me. But I temper that need by dreaming up scenarios that may or may not even be within the realm of possibility.

I'll become a well-known travel writer, scholar, philosopher. I'll write a bestselling book. Then another. I'll be prolific because of the constant influx of inspiration from my travels and the amazing cast of characters I surround myself with. I'll excel in several different fields, change the way people think, expand the reach of rationalism and create a minimalism movement that will simultaneously drive my corporate sponsors crazy and increase demand for their premium lines of products and services.

While writing this I know that this should sound like a pipe-dream, and that I should be really skeptical about all of it, resigning myself ahead of time to achieving a mere fraction, a handful of watered-down goals which I'll accept, eating up the minor victories and then sitting down for a break in the La-Z-Boy of suburbia, making babies, having a couple different wives and experimenting with recreational drug use.

It's easy! And who wouldn't want easy after a lifestyle that is bound to be full of so many challenges?

But I don't feel this way. In fact, I have very little doubt that I can achieve all of it.

What's more, I could add to the list (and I have, mentally) and it still doesn't seem insurmountable. Is this a symptom of my crazy? Do I have some kind of Personal Fable Syndrome, where I'm the hero of a storyline that is being written by a disembodied voice, narrating my every adventure with a jaunty English accent and an ironic self-aware perspective?

Hard to say.

I do know that if I weren't doing this, I would probably be miserable. The relationship I was in, though fantastic, felt like it was slowly grinding to a halt, while my studio was becoming more and more lucrative (and bringing in less and less interesting work).

Los Angeles wasn't diminishing in variety or vastness, but I felt like I had tasted enough of it to know that I had found my favorite flavor, and even that particular dish would soon become tiresome.

I could have moved to another state in the US, maybe someplace with a lower cost of living, which would have allowed me to increase my material standards even further, which according to the modern myth of the American businessperson would increase my happiness, grant me all the prestige and sexual prowess and looks and lovers that any one person could ever want.

What a depressing thought, to have to depend on 'stuff' to feel happy and good about myself! Just writing it made my stomach clench up. Take it away. Move on.

The strange thing is I think I've converted my addiction for work into an addiction for change. I've found that in the past, change has always been very good for me, and I see no reason for that pattern to change (ha!).

Or maybe it's my love for the non-standard?

I've never dated the expected kind of girl, I've never worked the 'right' job or studied the correct material (corporate job and business school? I'll pass, thanks). This has put me in the position to have a fairly unique skill set that's incredibly marketable, a track record for dating really amazing women, and a stockpile of knowledge that allows me to easily integrate myself into almost any conversation, social group, or new situation.

What started out as a defensive mechanism—I hated competing, so I removed myself from most competitions by doing things that achieved the same ends but took place on a completely different kind of playing field—that became one of my greatest assets.

So that's the path that led me to this moment in time, sitting on this plane, alternating staring out the window at the clouds, daydreaming, typing away on this little netbook, and smiling back at the flight staff who keep bringing me water, though the rest of the passengers seem to only have gotten one round of their chosen beverage (I must look really thirsty), listening to bouncy, perky music, and trying to remember whether or not my sister knows the exact time I'll be touching down so she can pick me up.

I hope so.

Chapter 2: Porteños & Possibilities

10.01.2009 — Notebook Entry — My Apartment, Buenos Aires, Argentina

There's a beeping in the hallway as I lay facedown naked on my queen-sized bed.

Queen-sized. That was an important detail when I was looking for a place to rent. And I'll bet if the queen ever found out that her name was being applied to something larger-than-average she'd throw a queen-sized tantrum. Such is the vanity of royalty.

This is the second day in which I've awoken, ready to jump-start my morning, only to come up short immediately after going through my post-waking information-gathering routine.

The email is now checked, the new blog post has been advertised. The news has been read, the shower taken. And here I recline, listening to this damn beeping that I'm pretty sure is the cry of a faulty elevator, trying to convince myself that I'm in the right mood, the right mindset, to write this ebook that I've got outlined and ready.

All it will take is a little brute force; a little applied torque in the wrists so they can tippity-type away at the keyboard and make it say the right things. Clarify the opinions I've been ranting about for the past several months and put them into an easy-to-digest, bento-box format.

The hardest part about traveling so far has been the loneliness.

I didn't think it would be a problem, the most difficult part of living with someone else, for me, has always been the lack of alone time, but there's a difference between 'being alone' and 'being lonely.' I'm much more aware of that difference now.

I get excited every time I run out of water. An excuse to walk down the street to the store! Joy! I mentally jump up-and-down like a dog who has just heard the word 'walk' spelled out by his master.

I recognize this feeling, and I know I feel it because it's a chance, though slim, that I might meet someone. That somebody at the grocery store (the main chain is called 'Disco' here, which I imagine leads to many disappointed 70's dance enthusiasts) will see me and want to connect enough that they will take the time to break through the language barrier. Or maybe they'll speak English! They'll tell me if I was right in my assumption about what kind of milk is fat free and how the cartons of orange juice are supposed to be opened. Saved!

And this person will be a woman, because it's much easier for a guy to survive with one friend when that friend is a girl. And she'll be artsy and have a lot of friends and will know about the more interesting things to do around town and she won't have heard of the music I listen to, but I'll make her a mix CD and she'll love it. Just love it. We'll fall for each other and the sex will be great and we'll spend just enough time together that there's no pressure and still things to do when we want to do them.

We'll fall for each other even harder and be best friends who keep in touch long after I leave and she'll know if she wants to come visit me she's more than welcome and I'll know that I have a place to crash in Buenos Aires and there won't be any tears when I leave because we'll both know that life is a celebration and this is just the last bite of one slice of cake. The party is far from over and there's plenty of cake left.

But, of course, that's just naive fantasy. In all likelihood things will progress as they have been progressing. I'll continue to hang out with the same crowd (mostly expats from English-speaking countries) and continue to have the same sporadic, exciting situations, punctuated by the hum-drum, exciting-on-paper lifestyle that someone like me lives when most of their friends exist only on the computer, several time zones away. Always in a new environment, never a part of it. Always meeting people, seldom making connections. The food is different, the language is incomprehensible, but the biggest change is a lack of physical connections.

No matter how clever emoticons get, there's something patently unsatisfying about an e-hug. An e-kiss.

Beep.

Photos of Stones

There's a photo here on my computer of two girls on a rock-covered beach.

One has her arm swung back, preparing to side-chuck a choice stone into the ocean, hoping to get a few skips out of it before it's pulled to the bottom. The other girl is intently studying a particularly colorful and glossy specimen, back turned toward the ocean, completely engaged in finding the best handful of nature to pop in her bag as a souvenir.

I recall the three of us were on this beach because of a 12-or-so hour layover at a bus stop in the middle of nowhere, partway through our journey south from Mendoza, headed toward Ushuaia at the very southern tip of Tierra del Fuego in Argentina.

We exchanged a few words mere hours before unloading at the flea-speck town, so unlike the myriad unlucky singletons milling around at the bus station, hunting down likely locations to rest on their bags and doze until the next bus arrived, we had the group-inspired courage to go shambling down the dirt road, uncertain if we would find anything, but hoping for a restaurant or grocery store, or even a petrol station with snacks.

After weaving our way through blocks of dilapidated housing, we stumbled across a small pizza restaurant in the alley between two vacant, one-story office buildings. The place was empty, and the owner was thrilled when we each ordered a beer along with our pie. He tried out his broken English (which actually wasn't bad, all things considered), and before we left he told us he was "very so happy" that we had "come to eat much inside."

Bellies full of cheese, crispy crust, and watery beer, we headed toward what looked to be the combined downtown and waterfront area, passing three hardware stores and a hotel before deciding to give up on shopping and just make our way to the beach.

It was chilly by the water, but not unpleasantly so, and we ditched our jackets for greater range of motion as we fell into a routine of scanning the area around our feet, bending down to pick up a smooth stone, admiring it for a second, and then dropping it in favor of more lustrous treasure.

From a distance we must have looked a bit like those little toy birds, the ones that slowly-but-surely bend down to dip their beaks into a glass of water only to pop back up, before laboriously making their way back down again.

After an hour at the beach, we walked back inland toward the downtown area, intending to entertain ourselves at a small playground we had seen on our way to the surf.

There was evidence along the top of the swing set that it was once painted green, but most of the paint had long ago worn away, leaving a rusty grey hue, almost like an acidic ocean had flooded this area, stripping the poor playground equipment's flesh from its metallic bones.

As I arced back and forth on the swing, I looked out at the horizon and tried to count the number of blues contained in the continuum of ocean to sky. There were far too many involved in the spectacular gradient looking back at me to count— thirty? fifty? one hundred thousand?—but before I could settle on a number, my attention was completely pulled away by the sound of the waves, which were more deafening now than when I was right up next to them, chucking stones into their depths.

Eventually we headed back into town to find a bathroom and ended up stopping in the lobby of a hotel we had passed earlier. We ordered drinks and took turns using the bathroom, brushing waxy teeth and washing grimy faces before applying some necessary deodorant and fussing with wind-whipped hair.

At this point, after 16 hours on a bus and five more in this little town, anything we could do to avoid looking like drifters with ill-intent was a step in the right direction.

Bags nestled in the corner, coffee on the table, we discussed our lives back home: how different they were from existence in this little town in this big country in this strange hemisphere with these unfamiliar sites, sounds, smells, and horizons.

One of my companions was English, and she had been teaching in a few different Argentine towns, but was now unemployed and planning to head home.

The other was Australian and started by regaling us with tales of giant spiders and other beasts that lived near her house outside of Brisbane. She was enjoying a gap year of sorts, taking a break from school to explore the world. She planned to leave Argentina around the same time I did, though her path until departure was undetermined.

We finished our drinks and slowly walked back to the bus station, where we sat down in a grassy patch in front of the building, reclining against our bags. The English girl produced a tiny set of collapsible speakers from her backpack and we took turns plugging in our iPods, telling stories related to the songs as they came on. We did this for the next six hours.

Looking at this photo, some details from that day are etched clearly in my mind, but some have faded away, leaving remnants, if anything, of what else happened, what else I learned about my comrades of convenience, what sights we saw while waiting out in front of that bus station.

And that's travel, isn't it?

A series of important events, worn down by time into digestible stories. The parts most interesting to whomever is listening are the parts you remember most clearly, while things that may have been vital at the time become a footnote or are completely forgotten.

But still, there are the snapshots left in your brain to go with the ones on your computer.

Clumps of knowledge you can't quite weave into the tale, but that make the experience real for *you*, the person who lived it. The texture of the table cloth in the hotel cafe. The tang of the cheese on the pizza in the tiny restaurant. The slipperiness of the stones and the creak of the swing and the pitch of each girl's voice as she spoke about her home, her family, her travel experiences.

The digital photos we keep do the same thing: they punctuate a given moment with extra importance *because* it's a moment frozen in time and remembered, not because that moment was more impactful than the one immediately before or after it.

Chance, as much as anything, plays a role in how we remember certain experiences and what we take away from them.

All we can do is try our best to take a lot of photos and tell a lot of stories to increase the odds we'll capture and retain the good ones.

The First Lady

I met Kara shortly after arriving in Buenos Aires.

She contacted me through an invite-only social network called A Small World and welcomed me to the city, though she herself had only been there a week. She invited me to come exploring with her and we walked around town, grabbed a few glasses of orange juice at a cafe, and meandered over to the Recoleta Cemetery.

Please note:

- If you want to order an orange juice in Argentina, ask for a *jugo de naranja*. Then smile and pretend you know more words than just those few.

- Kara is the kind of gal who has been showing her photography in galleries since she was maybe 12, and she won Woman Photographer of the Year at the Venice International Photographic Competition in 2005. She does not, however, enjoy having people she's just met take her picture (trust me).

- There's a sex worker bar not far from the Recoleta Cemetery. It's actually right across the street. It's a pretty obvious sex-trade dive, but it's also the only place open some nights. I think this bar, along with all the other houses of ill-repute nearby, directly correlate with the number of hotels in the vicinity that attract business tourists. Just sayin'.

- Kara has an English accent like the Queen of England. More on this in a moment.

The Cemetery houses some of the most elaborate tombs I've ever seen.

The sheer enormity of some of them is astounding, while others were clearly meant to be the stylish belles of the afterlife ball. Many are obviously incredibly expensive and also incredibly tasteless, while others seemed to have been built by eclectic art historians intent on stealing statuary and aesthetic pieces from just about every period in history.

Probably the most famous resident of the Cemetery (thanks to Hollywood and Madonna) is Eva Perón, of Evita ("Don't cry for me Argentinaaaa!"), whose tomb is significantly simpler than its neighbors. The cemetery is so enormous that there are blocks and neighborhoods inside it, but because Peron's final resting place is constantly surrounded by crowds of tourists and school children, it's easy to find.

Please note:

- There's one tomb shaped like a small, modern pyramid. Pharaohs and Louvre, eat your hearts out.
- On this first trip to the Cemetery, few other people were around (it was cloudy and looked like rain), so Kara and I had the place almost to ourselves. Stray cats are *everywhere*, though, so I guess you're never totally alone in such a place. They apparently eat the rats that go after the corpses, but the look on those little *gatos'* faces said that they had tasted human flesh, too, and that if I didn't pet them, they would taste it again.
- It's amazing to me how often people with a lot of money are willing to spend it on truly ugly things. It's not always the case, but certainly more frequent than I imagine most of them would like to think. I guess when you walk into an expensive clothier or

car lot (or in this case, tomb-store), you expect that the people there will tell you what really looks good and what actually looks bad, but self-editing is necessary for all economic classes, folks.

Kara told me about the farm her family lives on in Sussex, and about how she's decided to travel in search of meaning and inspiration.

When I heard farm, I assumed she came from a quaint area as part of a friendly (based on her demeanor), fairly middle-class family. There would be a pond, some cows, and lots of grass.

I was later informed by a few different English friends that, based on her accent and where her family is from, Kara is actually quite posh. Blue-blooded was another term that came up. I knew these words, but based on their reactions, I got the impression they meant something more when used by Brits than Americans.

Please note:

- There seem to be a whole lot of English folk in Argentina, but I may be biased since the group I fell in with introduced me to so many. I think the Brits do like to get out into the world a bit more than residents of many other countries, though.

- As I understand it, being blue-blooded refers to coming from a good or historically significant family, while posh means that you're high-society ('HiSo' as they say in Bangkok), and likely wealthy. As a Yank, the whole concept of blue-bloodedness is funny to me, but I assume it would probably be more important to someone who came from a Boston-based political family.

- I can't tell you how many people I've met since I started traveling who were looking for themselves, or for inspiration, or for what they *really* want to do with their lives, etc. Seldom do you hear people are looking for love, but that tends to happen more on the road than you would think. Also, a lot of these people are CEOs, lawyers, and doctors, completely worn out by their jobs and all swearing they've discovered their new love (horseback riding, yoga, kite-boarding, womanizing, etc) and won't be going back. Many don't.

- I always picture farms as having cows and grass and ponds. If you say the word 'organ farm,' the image that rolls through my head is six parts hilarious, four parts disturbing.

I hung out with Kara frequently throughout my stay in Argentina until we both left the country (she moved back to England for a bit, then Italy, and then to Israel, while I headed off to New Zealand). We still reminisce online, keeping in touch until our next in-person adventure.

Kara was the very first friend I made after I started traveling, and like with so many things, when it comes to platonic travel-buddies you never forget your first experience together (or the many details that go with it).

Desert Islanding

Dependence Dependent

"But how can you live with only 50 things in the WHOLE WORLD? I would die without my (*insert favorite thing here*)."

As someone who is experimenting with extreme Minimalism (basically stripping away the possessions, activities, and relationships that don't matter to me so I have more time, energy, and resources to spend on the ones that do), I hear sentiments like this a lot. Some blanch at the thought of living so simply. Some actually get offended and try to convince me I'm wrong, or a bad person for trying to live with less. Others have no response at all (but they're usually drunk and ogling someone across the room, so I chalk it up to distraction).

It's a topic that gets peoples' attention, though, and with good reason. The wealthy world thrives on consumerism, and the poorer world is quickly catching up or surpassing us in dedication to that philosophy. When someone steps out of those bounds (or appears to), it's as if they slapped you in the face with some kind of holy book (the IKEA catalog?). Sacrilege!

I'm not a fanatic, though. I like stuff. I like to have a fancy computer and a high-quality pen for scribbling in my heavily-branded sketchbook.

Stuff isn't inherently bad.

I do, however, recognize that dependence (especially a personal dependence on 'stuff' in order to feel confident or capable) can be very bad, and I learned this the hard way my senior year of college.

Climbing the Tallest Tree

I was dual-majoring in Graphic Design and Illustration, and pursuing a bunch of different minors in random subjects. I was also working five different jobs, dating a girl that I had been seeing for over a year, and partying every weekend with a quirky collection of friends I loved.

I was living in a two-bedroom apartment a few blocks from downtown, and although the rent was very low by my current standards, by college-me standards it was quite high. I had all kinds of space I didn't need, a pool I never used, an extra parking spot, the works. I was also eating quite well, frequently going out and buying drinks for people. It was a good life.

There came a point, however, when things needed to change. The spark that lit the fire was when the Editor-in-Chief for a magazine I was working for decided he wasn't interested in hearing any more of my ideas. His reasoning? "If they were good ideas, surely someone else would already have done them. We should keep doing things the way we have been and outwork our competition."

As a result of that discussion I left the magazine along with a colleague. We had decided to show him how it was done by starting our own publication.

Sure, the only publishing experience we had between us was her design work for a newspaper and my journalism education and columnist gigs, but hell, a good idea is a good idea! Let's go get 'em!

And we did. Though she ended up having to leave the project before the real festivities began, the magazine became a reality, complete with advertisers and a whole lot of work. We knew, though, it wouldn't be enough just to have a good product. People had to know about it before it could become truly popular and successful.

A plan was devised! An epic plan, which required assistance from three close friends with varying skill sets.

Working together, we planned a combination concert and fashion show, featuring different genres of music, along with multiple designers and boutiques showing off their work on a catwalk-stage.

It would be huge! And did I mention epic?

When the night of the event rolled around, it was the highlight of my college career. Not only did people show up, people showed up in *droves*. It was a big success, and enough money came in to overpay the bands and cover all of our costs. Awareness was sky-high for the new publication.

For a while, I became a bit of a local celebrity; the kid who had put together the big event. I was not only getting trash-talked by rival publications, but also congratulated by some of the writers who penned the hit pieces over drinks after work hours.

People thought the project was cool, and by association I became cool. This was a new experience for me. It felt good.

After the fanfare, anticipation, and success of the first event and issue, expectations were high for issue number two.

We had several advertisers on the fence, but they were happy with the turnout of the first event. If I could do that again, they said, they'd be fully on board and willing to commit for six months or more. That would show staying power, and with the number of people they'd seen carrying my mag around town, they felt it would herald my magazine's real coming out.

Knowing this, and wanting to one-up myself (a constant endeavor of mine), I started reaching out to groups within my University and some local governmental services. A few days after the first event, I was in meetings with local politicians and other leaders in an effort to reserve the city square of the downtown area for a massive concert unlike anything my college town had seen before.

We got the space, we got sponsors (including MTV's Rock the Vote), we got food and press and advertising. Everyone wanted to be involved, and we let them take part in some way or another. This was going to be a big pie, and they could all have a piece so long as they helped me bake it.

During this time I quit two of my jobs—the ones that paid the most, but took up most of my time—so I could focus more on the magazine and the event. I slept three or four hours a night (when I slept), but I got all of my class work done, and spent the rest of my time fielding phone calls from collaborators and giving instructions to the trio of friends who had helped put together the first event.

I was on a high. I had momentum. I felt strong, capable, and invincible.

Hitting Every Branch on the Way Down

The day of the event, as I was loading equipment into my car to take downtown, I looked up at the horizon and my jaw dropped in horror as chunky, black clouds rolled in to cover the city. I mouthed some profanity and hopped into the car, racing to the square, hoping someone there would be able to reassure me the storm would miss us.

When I arrived a few minutes later, it was all over. The rain was coming down torrentially, and I could barely see anything through the windshield of my car. A smattering of volunteers were scurrying around the square, doing their best to pack expensive equipment into rented, white vans before it was damaged by the deluge. I pulled over to the side of the road and put my head in my hands. No. Oh no.

I took a deep breath, pulled myself together, and reached for my phone to call the loyal friends who had helped set everything up to see if anyone had solutions for me.

"No," one of them said. "The weather forecast said it was supposed to be sunny all day today. We had no reason to plan for this. We should call the radio stations to tell them it's been called off, though."

Shit, the radio stations. And the TV networks. And all the University clubs who were helping out, organizing transportation from campus and security for the event. And the bands. Everyone needed to be notified the event was being called off due to the bad weather.

After sending out some texts and leaving a few voicemails, delivering the bad news to my media contacts and the school's club leaders, the last few calls I made were to theaters and other venues as I scrambled to find an indoor location where I could move the event. I finally got in touch with the owners of a nice, big gallery a few blocks from the square, and we rescheduled the concert to take place there a few days later.

Unfortunately, a lot of our credibility—nay, *my* credibility—had been used up while planning the event for the square.

New posters had to be printed, new press releases for the local media, new deals with sponsors. Most of the companies involved weren't able to recommit to another day, and many were upset their previous efforts would go unrewarded (especially those who donated food that would go to waste). I assured them they would still be thanked at the new event, even if they couldn't contribute further.

When the first band finally went on stage, there was no stage. When I looked out into the audience, there was no audience.

A half-dozen people showed up, and only two of the bands bothered to attend. There was no free food, no giant vinyl posters, no reporters (thank god). It was a mess. I was horrified. I wanted to die.

Issue two of my magazine floundered. It was a solid piece of work, but there was little exposure, as most of the shops who committed to have it distributed pulled out after their sponsorship of the most recent event was wasted.

I had one advertiser for the next issue and I found myself in a very precarious spot.

I had a high cost of living and only half the income I'd been earning before I refocused on the magazine. Though I had never been rich, for a long time I had been better off than most of my friends because of all the jobs I was working. Suddenly, I was something I had never been before: worryingly short on money.

Gilliganning

For a while I tried to keep living the way I was, surviving on what amounted to starvation rations when I wasn't out on the town, spending money I didn't have when I was.

I knew this could only work for so long. I was subsisting on eggs and water (the two cheapest things I could find), and I couldn't even afford to take my girlfriend out to dinner. It hurts to fall, and it hurts more to fall from a great height you had only recently reached.

I learned so much from this particular failure, but one tidbit that didn't fully crystallize until several years later was this: dependence on a specific income, a piece of technology, or a person or group of people in order to be successful and have a good life is a horribly precarious position to be in. I realized if I needed these things, and couldn't live without them, then my life wasn't built on *my* success or talent or brains, but on external sources of motive power. So many 'if's.

New questions cropped up any time I thought about taking on a new challenge.

If I couldn't do good work on *any* computer, was I really that talented?

If I couldn't have fun when I wasn't out drinking and eating expensive food, was I really happy?

If I couldn't live without a certain person in my life, was I really living?

The only way to stop these questions was to seek out some answers, and the result of that search is what you see today: a guy who has streamlined the unnecessary possessions, activities, and people from his life so only the most vital remain.

Minimalism does not mean owning as little as possible. It's cutting out the things you don't care about, that you don't *need*, so you can invest more of yourself in the stuff you're passionate about.

This is why I decided to experiment with owning extremely few possessions. Doing so allows me to clearly and honestly answer that burning question: what would you bring if you were stranded on a desert island?

Traveling allows me to remove myself from the patterns of everyday life and forced camaraderie. I don't have to see anyone, ever, if I don't want to. So who do I invest my time and effort trying to stay in touch with? This is another part of that same desert island question: whom would you bring with you?

Finally, by working for no one but myself, I have the freedom to skip the nine-to-five job, and trade the office for the open road. This means I can figure out *what* I would do while on that island.

These seem to be questions most people have never asked themselves, or at least haven't answered honestly. I made a list of essentials when I started plotting my new lifestyle and truth be told, it was very different from what I actually own today. What we think we need isn't always what makes us whole.

Sometimes we have to fall back down to earth, and suffer a hard landing, to achieve some semblance of clarity.

Astrology &
Prophylactics

Aries Luck

It was a beautiful night in Buenos Aires when I met Alfonso and Sofia. A beautiful night for a rooftop party.

After wandering the streets a few districts over from mine, I found myself walking through the open door of an apartment building. Once inside, I became acutely aware that (1) I didn't know anyone and (2) I didn't speak Spanish. Clearly, the night was either going to rule or suck. I hoped for the former, but planned for the latter.

I made my way up the stairs toward the roof where I could hear some disco-funk music and see lights casting silhouettes of dancing bodies on the door ahead. As soon as I reached the top and walked out onto the rooftop, I was nearly knocked down by a throng of revelers. I stepped backward toward the stairs to get my bearings and avoid getting lost in the fray.

My eyes drifted back and forth over the visual cacophony, picking out individuals where I could.

There was a jovial-looking man in a checkered suit-jacket and a Romani-esque party-girl with a penchant for dirty dancing. A dozen feet away was a gorgeous, petite, Asian girl chatting with a very tall German guy in a suit. Further back, a small cluster of musicians were sitting at their stations behind their instruments, probably done for the night, since their power cords were coiled and protective coverings were stretched over the drums.

Just as I had mentally prepared myself to slide through the mass of flailing limbs and drunken smiles toward what I had hoped was the drink table, I was approached by a lanky and wild-eyed *Porteño* (a local of Buenos Aires) who stepped right in front of me and started asking questions in Spanish.

He must have read my confused look to mean English would be necessary, because he smoothly transitioned between languages and introduced himself. "I'm Alfonso," he said, shaking my hand excitedly. "What is your name? Where are you from? Do you have a drink?"

I answered his questions, and upon hearing the answer to the final one, he said "This is not right, I will get you something," and pulled me into the crowd. We surfaced on the other side of the roof near a small table with an assortment of liquors and juices, though I had to step over piles of discarded plastic cups littering the ground in front of it to get there.

After a few minutes of conversation, it became clear Alfonso was hitting on me. I casually slipped an ex-girlfriend reference into a response to one of his questions and he reacted as soon as the words 'girlfriend' rolled off my tongue. "Have you met Sofia?" he asked, and was off in a flash to find her..

A few drinks and a half-dozen language-barrier-brief conversations later, Alfonso coalesced out of the crowd, dragging with him the cute Asian gal I had noticed earlier.

Seeing her up close, it was obvious she was actually a *Porteña* with slightly Asiatic features and was just as stunning up close as she was from a distance.

She smiled, reached out her hand and pulled me into a small area that had been cleared for dancing. I didn't know any of the local moves, but she was going freeform, which I could do. An hour later we collapsed against a wall, and she slid over to me and asked what my sign was.

"Aries, uh, I think."

"Me too," she said seductively, only slurring a little, though it could have just been her accent. "How old are you?"

"24."

"Well I'm 26, and that means I get to decide what we do next."

She pulled my head down for a kiss and we made out. A lot.

My thoughts simplified into this: Argentina fucking rocks.

The Games We Play

I've never been big on playing games in relationships. Do you wait two days before calling? Three?

Who cares? I say if you want to hang out with someone, call them. If they give you their number they want to hear from you, and the more time you waste playing games the less time you have to enjoy their company. Life's too short for that kind of nonsense.

That's what I *thought*, at least, until I called Sofia the afternoon after the rooftop party to see if she wanted to grab a cup of coffee.

"No, I am very busy today. *Lo siento.*"

"It's no problem," I replied. "Maybe sometime later in the week?"

"No, I think this week is very busy too."

"Got it. No worries. It was a pleasure to meet you, and let me know if you find yourself with any free time!"

I was bummed; was I really misreading her signals that badly? But I got the message, talking to her on the phone. Not interested. At least she had been quick about it, not leading me on after the one drunken night.

A week later I had lunch with Tali, another woman I had met at the rooftop party, who also happened to be the owner of the roof in question.

Tali was a tall, skinny blonde Brit who could somehow drink like a fish without suffering any negative physical consequences the next day. We knocked back a few bottles of wine over pasta at a sidewalk cafe halfway between our respective flats, and she wasted no time jumping in for the latest gossip as soon as the first glass was poured.

"So how did things go with Sofia?"

"I thought it went really well! I got a good vibe and she seemed to feel the same, but I called her a week ago and she didn't seem interested. *C'est la vie* I guess."

"You did *what*? Colin, darling, how could you be so stupid?"

Then, with the patience of a parent explaining the basics of life to a six-year-old, Tali told me how dating works in Argentina.

First, I was told, you find a girl you like and you aggressively pursue her, in some cases going so far as to grab or kiss her neck, to make it clear that you're interested (and if she says 'no,' that just means 'try harder').

After you get her number, wait two or three weeks before calling, to show that you don't *need* her and to let her simmer a little and wonder if you're going to call at all.

When you finally do call her, make it plain you had a good time and you'd like to meet at a specific place, on a specific day, and at a specific time. This shows her you can take control and are not afraid to be a man.

If she can't make it for some reason, move on. She clearly doesn't care enough to change her plans for you and she isn't worth your effort.

If she does meet you as instructed, you have to slip subtle insults into the conversation, little comments about having liked her hair better the last time you saw her, or about how she seems a little uncoordinated and probably can't dance very well, so that she has something to prove next time you see her.

"I didn't make these rules," she explained, "but this is how it works."

"But I don't get it, why would anyone want this? Won't that just make women hate men and make it more difficult for men to get women?"

"Yes, but the way I understand it, it works because they thrive on that sort of violent passion. And sometimes it's literally violent. I have girlfriends who tell me they like a guy who they can hate so much they want to fuck him."

I was flabbergasted, but after questioning a few locals I had met about the accuracy of this information, it checked out. I spent a good deal of time just sitting on my bed, going over that night at the rooftop party and thinking, "How the hell do people come up with this shit?"

Rough Translation

Another week passed, and I found myself sitting at a table in a semi-fancy bar/restaurant with Tali, Sofia, and my good friend Javier (a *porteño* photographer I met through Tali).

We discussed local politics and caught up on each other's lives. All the while, Sofia kept eyeing me and smiling from across the table.

I sipped at my beer nervously and assumed the only reason she had come out with us was that Tali had explained to her I was Argentine-dating ignorant, and convinced her I should get another shot.

Unfortunately, I didn't know what stage we were at, or what that meant I should do. I wasn't going to start hurling insults at her, so what then? Hell, even if I *wanted* to hurl insults at her, I wouldn't have known how with my incredibly meager Spanish vocabulary. My options were limited.

When the ladies grabbed their clutches and took a trip to the *baño*, I explained the situation to Javier, who calmly listened and then said, "Okay, I think I know what you should say." He then recited of a stream of words that could have been Spanish or Klingon for all the sense they made to me.

"No, no, Javi, that's not going to work. Here!" I handed him a napkin. "I'll find a pen."

I spun around and ran to the bar, where I borrowed a pen from the bartender and got back to my seat right before the girls exited the loo.

As Tali continued telling a story she had started before heading to the bathroom, Javier jotted-down and translated a few choice phrases he thought would help me succeed on the square, multi-ply, lightly-textured *servilleta*.

When he was through, he surreptitiously handed the napkin to me under the table and I took a look when the conversation allowed.

It said:

Se que no tuvimos oportunidad de hablar, pero realmente me gusta conocerte mas. Me pareces una person increíble.

Below, there was a rough English translation:

I know we didn't have much time to know each other, but I'm really looking forward to it. I think you are really amazing.

Close enough!

A few hours later, Tali and Javier left Sofia and me alone to have a few more drinks on the front patio of the bar. As we got up to leave after finishing our drinks, I offered to walk Sofia to her apartment (there's a good deal of crime in Buenos Aires, and she was a very small person), and she accepted my offer.

As we were walking, she grabbed hold of my hand and we both smiled, enjoying the cool night air after a hot day and alcohol-filled night. We crossed a railroad track and saw some bonfires a mile or so away, down the tracks to our right. I tried to figure out how to ask if that was common, but when I tried she shrugged her shoulders and shook her head; she didn't understand.

When we arrived at her place, she thanked me for walking her and asked if I wanted to come inside and have a cup of tea. As she asked, she pulled my head down by the collar of my shirt and kissed me. When the kiss ended, we paused, forehead to forehead, our noses almost touching. I smiled and said "Why not?"

The apartment was small and a little ramshackle, but so were most apartments in that part of town, so I wasn't caught off guard. Sofia quickly put a few dirty dishes in the sink and started to heat some water for tea. She then pulled me into her bedroom, pushed me onto a beanbag chair and started to take off her shirt.

At this point I'm thinking: Yes! Go Argentina!

But shortly thereafter another thought sprang to the forefront: Oh wait! I don't know this girl very well! And I don't have any condoms!

I looked around to see if she might have a stash somewhere in view, but my quick survey came up short. I wondered if she had them hidden somewhere, and would pull them out when needed. She took her shirt all the way off and went in for mine.

The foreplay was quick and rough, and by the time most of our clothes were off I was starting to get a little concerned that perhaps there *wasn't* a secret stash of prophylactics. I flashed back to a few (incredibly uncomfortable) similar situations I had been through in college and I was worried, just like before, I'd have to figure out how to tell a hot girl who was ready to go that we couldn't have sex.

Traveling long-term is funny, because it tends to evoke equal parts xenophobia and xenophilia (respectively, fear and attraction to people from other parts of the world). There's a mystique about the men and women who spend their lives hopping from place to place, and depending on who you talk to, these globetrotters are either the sexiest people you'll ever come across or germ-carrying petri dishes who are best avoided.

Those who fall into the latter category usually reference STIs as a major reason to avoid travelers, because they 'hop from port to port.' I haven't personally come across much discrimination because of this (generally false) assumption, but I know a few people (guys and girls) who have, and I do all I can to make sure it remains just a rumor.

This is a big part of why I'm not a fan of one night stands. How can you tell if someone is telling you the truth when they say they've been tested recently, or that they don't have anything you can catch? How can you judge someone's personal integrity, especially when it deals with something so specific, based on just one date? You can't, and this is why when I looked up at the beautiful Argentine woman straddling me on the beanbag chair in her apartment, all I could think was 'this really shouldn't happen, this is a huge risk.'

Thankfully, as we rounded second base, she started nibbling on my ear and whispered "Do you have a condom?"

I paused before saying, "No, actually, I don't. I didn't realize anything was going to happen tonight," but before I could finish my sentence she pulled away and looked me dead in the eyes, as if to make sure she heard me right.

"No?"

"No, sorry. I really didn't realize..." but she was off of me as soon as I said 'no,' and started to pull her pants on.

I sighed in resignation but I couldn't really blame her. How could I not know? Why didn't I come prepared? Or at least prepared for the possibility?

I reached down to pick up my shirt, and Sofia was already fully dressed and back in the kitchen, picking the kettle up off the stove from where it had been shrieking for god knows how long.

I steeled myself for awkwardness as I finished putting my clothes back on, but when I walked into the kitchen, she handed me a cup of tea she had already poured and sipped on hers, making small-talk as if nothing had happened.

She gave me a kiss on the lips as I left her apartment, but I knew I had blown it a second time, and I got the impression that Sofia didn't give third chances.

I walked outside and realized it was a beautiful night.

I looked around to make sure no one was laying in wait to rob me, took a deep breath, and began my long walk home.

Israelis in Ushuaia

Blind Travelers & Cow Dolphins

Some dolphins are spotted like cows. Moo.

It's actually kind of cool that I know this: the day I encountered such dolphins, I could barely see.

I was on a shuttle boat taking me and a busload full of passengers (along with our bus) from Argentine Patagonia to Chilean Patagonia. This, apparently, was the fastest way to make it from Cordoba down to Ushuaia at the southernmost tip of Argentina, and it was the first time I had ridden on a boat that carried a bus *and* its passengers across a body of water.

I had been on the road for nearly 24 hours, and partway through the trip my eyes had become quite irritated, so I removed my contacts and put on my glasses, hoping after a few hours of sleep and some clean, delicious oxygen, my eyes would be good to heft those little lenses again.

I couldn't have been more wrong.

After resting, my eyes became even more irritated, and I was unable to get the contacts aligned with my retinas without immense pain.

I tried to put them back in for what felt like ages, then gave up and decided to let my eyes air-out for a few days, lest they should still be in bad shape for Christmas, which was a week later.

And so it was that I found myself on a boat, the wind flapping through my hair and the horizon a blur of beautiful hues, unable to clearly see anything past my outstretched arm because the lenses in my glasses were an old prescription. I squinted to make out the faces of my fellow passengers and I photographed the landscape the best I could.

My sight deficit wasn't too big a problem on the bus, since just about everything and everyone pertinent to my world was close enough for me to see. But outside, in the open air, with all kinds of novel sights and sounds, I felt helpless, afraid to look at people and make eye contact in case I should accidentally shoot someone a meaningful glance and unknowingly make an enemy by not returning their friendly nod.

I could hear the dolphins though, and I was one of the few on the boat able to snap a photograph of them riding in the ship's wake.

The photo turned out remarkably clear, though at the time all I could tell was there was *something* going on down below, and I heard someone behind me say the word 'dolphin,' so I inferred a bit about what might be happening.

After another day of nearly-blind bus travel, I finally arrived in Ushuaia and hopped a taxi with a friend I had made on the bus. We hurried to escape the biting, frosty sleet/rain (slain?) that was cutting through our jackets like tiny razors and freezing our hands, making it difficult to get enough *pesos* from our pockets to pay the driver.

I spent a good deal of the first few days in bed, walking around just enough to find a small supermarket to buy wine and cheese (two staples of the Argentine hostel-circuit diet) before heading back to my miniature sanctuary.

And a sanctuary it was.

The hostel had decently speedy WiFi, a relatively comfortable bed, and heated floors; a pleasant contrast to the freezing cold winds and periodic rainfall outside. I left the door open and listened to it swing slowly back and forth with the steady port-town breeze as I got some writing done and set up Skype calls with friends and family who were celebrating the holidays back in the States.

Three days later, just two days before Christmas, I put my contacts back in and there was no pain. And just that quickly, I was a different person.

Sight for the Blind

Up until Contact Lenses Reapplication Day, I had been moping around a fair bit. In fact, the people at the front desk wondered (in front of me; they must have assumed I didn't speak any Spanish, but I had picked up enough to get the gist of what was being said) if I was sick or just boring. As soon as I could see, I started making friends with everyone. I recruited hostel-mates to join me at the docks to take photos and to wander around town, searching out the best *medialunas* and *alfajores*. I was graced with flirty glances and comments from the hostel staff.

I was *alive* again, because I could see clearly once more. The landscape took my breath away, and I found myself going out every night with the girl I had met on the bus, both of us trying to bribe ship captains with beer in hopes of getting work and free passage aboard their Antarctica-bound vessels (the trip would normally cost between $4-10k USD).

We were unsuccessful in becoming sailors, but we did become the unofficial king and queen of Dublin, the most popular Irish pub in Ushuaia (believe it or not, in a town of about 60,000 people at the end of the world, there are *two* Irish pubs) for a week or so.

Later, I befriended some German backpackers camping their way around the country, and we visited the Tierra Del Fuego State Park, hiking around old Native American huts and trying to pet wild horses while admiring the stunning landscape (this is the only part of South America, by the way, that has natural views that are competitive with New Zealand and Iceland). My shoes were destroyed during the hike, but it was totally worth it.

Tourist, Trapped

On Christmas Eve, when there seemed to be *nothing* going on in the tiny town of Ushuaia, I ended up falling for a tourist trap. Something I very seldom do.

I paid my 200 pesos (about $50 USD) and hopped into a small van with about a dozen other travelers. We drove from my hostel to a rundown warehouse on the other side of town and met up with about 80 other people who had been similarly hoodwinked.

As a party, it was pathetic.

The food was cold, the selection was piddly and quality was clearly not the focus. For the first hour, I sat with a group of Europeans, ate crappy pasta, and took turns verbally despising the pricks who had convinced us this would be the party of the century.

A half-hour later, however, we had imbibed enough drinks that things were looking up. Suddenly, it didn't matter we had been tricked. It was a good joke on us! We started dancing and got the occupants of a few other tables (who were business travelers, based on their attire) to join us. Soon, the whole room was bopping to the music, and those who weren't up and cutting a rug with us were wishing they had the guts to.

It was around this time that a new group of people filtered into the warehouse. This one was clearly organized, consisting of people who knew each other pre-Ushuaia, and their presence poured oil on the fire. I quickly discovered they were Israelis who had just finished their compulsory military duty and were taking time off to travel the world before going back home for University or work.

Drinks were bought, names were exchanged, a little making out might have occurred.

Around 1am I left the warehouse with a triple-handful of Israelis, and instead of catching the shuttles back to our hostels, we decided it would be fun to look for a club.

We trekked around town, climbing steep hills away from the docks, perusing the tourist district, but nothing was open.

We eventually found a small club with a crowd of people out front, but no one inside. I asked the bouncer why everyone was lingering outside instead of going in, and was told the cover was 100 pesos per person, more than anyone out there could easily afford. I looked at the bouncer and then at the group of 17 people (15 of whom were young women) I had with me, and told him, "Listen, if you let us in for free, we will buy drinks all night. Not only that, but if you have these girls in there, all these guys standing around will pony up the dough to come inside as well. Why would they pay a cover charge if there's nobody inside for them to buy drinks for?"

After 15 minutes or so of negotiation, and a few minutes for the bouncer to talk to the club's manager, they finally decided they would let *me* inside for free, but not anyone else (I have no idea how they could possibly think that was a good compromise). I told them being the only person in their club would make for one lonely party, then left, my group falling in step behind me.

At this point it was clear nothing else was open. We started walking back toward our respective hostels, and where the road split (their hostel one way, mine the other), one of the girls said, "Aww come on, you should come back to our room! We'll have a good time, I promiiiise!" If she could have inserted a winky-smiley emoticon in real life, she would have.

But I knew my limit, and the alcohol from the party was finally hitting me hard, so I told them I would love to, but I would probably just fall asleep and wouldn't be any fun. I would, however, love to see them tomorrow if they were game.

They said they would see me the next night. When I arrived at Dublin the next day, however, they weren't anywhere to be found. One of the guys from their group was there, and I asked him about the girls.

"Oh yeah," he said. "They left yesterday. Turns out their boyfriends who are touring around up north found out they were flirting with other guys and demanded that they leave early and go spend New Year's up there with them."

I thanked him for the info, bought him one of Dublin's trademark green beers and saluted him with a clink of the glass and a 'l'chayim!' before leaving the bar, heading back to my hostel and silently reminding myself it was probably for the best.

Some stories are meant to end early.

The Morning After

Oh shit, my head.

Ouch ouch ouch, goddamn that hurts. Stomach is lurching uncomfortably, too.

I had too much to drink last night. A bit too much. More than a bit. I don't know how much I drank last night. Why did I do that?

I think it started with the vodka. No one should ever give me vodka and tell me to make my own drink. That's just a recipe for, well, a really bad drink, but also for not remembering part of the evening. What happened last night?

I need to eat something.

Why do I keep drinking? I honestly don't even know why. It's not like I particularly enjoy drinking screwdrivers and such. Wine can be fun, or a good beer, but liquor is just...

It's a bad idea. Really bad. When I close my eyes the room spins a little bit, and it's 3pm.

My studio is small, but comfortable and well-designed.

One wall consists of windows facing an internal alleyway, and I always wonder what would happen if I fell out and got stuck on the ground a few stories below.

Would there be a door? There would have to be, right? Maybe just a ladder. Or a rope. I should really carry a small rope with me everywhere I go, in case I find myself in that kind of situation. I should be able to fashion some kind of crude grappling hook from whatever is lying around, but maybe I could find a collapsible one online somewhere.

Food? No. I still don't think I can take anything, though it would probably help.

Am I still drunk? No, probably just so sick and poisoned that I can't quite focus on anything too close to my eyes. It's 3:15pm and it's pitch black because I've got the Venetian blinds pulled and the drapes pulled over them to quash any bits of light that manage to make it through the first line of defense.

I can sleep all day if I want to! No, it's worse lying down. If I sit up and tilt my head forward just a little, hands resting on my knees, I don't feel quite as bad. I can almost relax. And think.

Alcohol is one of those things that have become sexy due to decades of ambitious branding. Drinking is for parties and dates and celebrations after baseball games (and during baseball games) and being a rebel and fitting in and getting laid and having it all. If you're not able to drink, what's the point? That's what life is all about, if everything and everyone is to be believed.

I have some pasta I can eat. I should just eat it.

I've only lost parts of a night once before, and that was in college. I was dating a girl who was an enthusiastic drinker, and as a result I started drinking quite a bit more for a while.

We were out at this place called The Jam, which was essentially a long hallway with a bar that spanned one wall, and a DJ booth at the end. There were a few tables, but they were always covered with spilled alcohol and olives. They were a tease more than anything. Stupid tables.

The Jam had one purpose: to get college kids totally hammered.

They had this deal where you could pay $5 at the door and get as many drinks as you wanted, though you could only have two at a time, so you had to pace yourself somewhat (ha!).

That night I had thirteen Long Island Ice Teas, and by the time the place closed, I was sitting with my girlfriend on the skeezy, black leather couch near the exit, trying to keep the room from spinning (that's something else that has only happened to me once before....nothing worse than 'the spinnies').

A friend of ours put us in a cab and paid the driver, and thankfully I only lived a few blocks away, but my girlfriend and I spent the better part of that night taking turns hugging the toilet, trying hard to throw up but mostly just feeling incredibly sick.

Ah, college.

But I'm a damn professional now. I do things. In other countries. I wear suit jackets, damnit, and here I am, naked and sick in Argentina, trying to figure out what transpired last night.

I'm told I went to a club, but I really don't remember. No blurry mental snapshots or anything, which is frustrating and a little disorienting. Did I do anything illegal? Probably not, but you never know.

I woke up in my friend's bed, but she and I were both fully-clothed, so I don't think any funny-business went down. There are a few photos up on Facebook of me wearing a friend's fake-mustache and enormous sunglasses, but other than that there doesn't seem to be any evidence of where I went, with whom, and whether or not I did anything I would regret.

What am I so worried about? I know who I am. I know what I believe in and how I operate. I know nothing too serious could of happened, and the biggest thing I probably have to worry about is embarrassing myself by being over-enthusiastic, shouting conversation at people or otherwise being a talkative drunk. It's not like I'm going to jump off a building or kill someone or start a coke habit or anything. I'll be fine and I am fine and I was fine. It was great. No worries.

But I am worried.

When you drink your prefrontal cortex loses access to certain signals and chemicals and lowers your inhibitions. This isn't terrible if you want to loosen up for a social situation, but if you block too many of these signals, you lose a lot of what makes you a civilized human being and become more beast than man.

Who's to say what someone is capable of when they've lost all inhibitions?

What *wouldn't* they do?

If I drink myself stupid, even for just a night, could it dramatically change the way I operate, leading to a very stupid decision that physically impairs me for life? Or that destroys someone else's life in some way?

Might I accidentally get married or drown a sack of puppies or buy real estate or get caught painting an eyepatch on a billboard-model's face?

I should drink more water. I should drink more water *every* day. I should be healthier, instead of just working out and trusting that will keep me fit. I've been eating so much pasta and pizza since I've been here I'll probably turn into ravioli if I don't stop soon. But damn, do I love Argentine pesto.

Ugh, okay, I shouldn't think of pesto. Almost lost it there. Not appealing to the palate right now. Need more water.

It's funny, actually, because I didn't start drinking until a long time after a lot of my friends.

I waited until I was 20 and only started drinking at all because I was kind of seeing a girl who I liked, but who I couldn't have a conversation with, due to our very different opinions about politics and religion and I guess life priorities in general.

She suggested one day we play a drinking game and I went along with it as if I had been drinking since I was a toddler. Too cool for school, that was me.

We both got drunk, words were said, and we didn't talk for a few days.

I should have known then that alcohol, though useful as a social tool, doesn't innately make anything good, it merely emphasizes what's already there. Bad stuff included.

If you're having a good time, a few drinks could make it better. If you're feeling down or not enjoying yourself, it's likely adding vodka or cheap beer into the mix will turn a crummy night crappy.

But I think that's probably true with anything we're sold as part of some escapist dream.

Trying to make things better from the outside-in is a lot more difficult than doing it from the inside-out, and it doesn't have the same resilience. Studies have shown that smiling can make you feel happier because of some kind of muscle-memory, brain-thing, but if you're confident, curious and feeling good, you can scowl all day long and still have a great time. Better to improve things overall than to just come up with slapdash solutions to problems as they arise.

I'm imagining how I must have felt before I started drinking last night.

I was healthy and strong and my body was operating perfectly. I could run a mile or dance a jig or just sit quietly, but I doubt I would have appreciated it. Seems I only take stock of this kind of thing when it's gone, which is a bit counterproductive.

I know these things—I know that I don't *need* to drink, or even want to sometimes—but I also know I will probably keep doing it.

I went the better part of a year without drinking alcohol recently and it saved me a good deal of money and was probably great for my health. I didn't miss it. On the other hand, I spent so much time explaining to people why I wouldn't drink with them that it got a little ridiculous.

All the effort it took to make clear I wasn't judging them for drinking when I was sticking to water, all the awkward glances and drunken rants from friends telling me they're embarrassed to be drunk in front of me while I stubbornly remained stone-cold sober. It added up. And here I am, back in the drunken saddle.

Life is full of these tradeoffs, and I like to think they lend a bit of theatrical drama to otherwise mundane everyday situations. Sure, you can be socially acceptable, but in order to do so you must ingest this poison along with everyone else. Have a good time. Cue the menacing music.

It's a bit like hazing new members on a sports team or in a fraternity; socially, people who have to suffer a bit to gain entrance to a group will value their membership a whole lot more than folks who are just let in, no muss, no fuss.

There are benefits to engaging in shared experiences, being able to act out, and letting down your guard completely. To drop the mask and show your friends who you really are while they do the same. That's the kind of thing that makes for tight bonds and great stories.

And yet, here I am thinking about all of this while my liver struggles to clean my blood, wishing I could muster the appetite to finish off the leftover pesto-ravioli I have in the fridge, and wondering if knowledge really is power, or if in some cases it's just like the paintings I'm staring at on my wall: interesting, but largely irrelevant to the function of the room and how I go about my day.

Or maybe I should stop looking at paintings and start making some, just as I should stop merely knowing things and start acting upon them. Knowing what's right for you is one thing, but doing something about it is a completely different story.

The Mysterious Joys of Travel

Stupid Bus

This bus ride has been hell.

It's been 60 hours since I left Buenos Aires for Lima, Peru, then Bogota, Colombia, then back to the States to spend a few weeks with friends and family. Since I boarded the bus that makes up the first leg of my journey, I've spent most of my time swatting flies and trying not to dehydrate.

I don't know how I ended up on the one crappy bus in Argentina.

Running tandem with us the whole way has been a super-lux, clean and fancy double-decker. The kind I've grown accustomed to since moving to South America. The food is good, the air conditioners work, and the seats are comfortable. You can recline in them! You can sleep! No flies!

But this bus...oh this bus.

I distract myself by looking out the window and imagining what it would be like to live in the places we pass by. It's a difficult exercise. It's not the language or the culture that's hard to wrap my head around, it's the poverty.

As a white kid who grew up in the suburbs, first in Northern California and then Missouri, I knew I hadn't exactly had it rough. My family has never been wealthy, but we have always been able to afford food. We took trips sometimes. We had video games. Books. Electricity.

Some of these towns, if you can even call them that, don't seem to have electricity, or at least they don't at night. Their water comes from wells and their food comes from carts.

Everywhere I look there are jarring reminders of a more familiar lifestyle that emphasize the surrealistic situation for me: Coca-Cola signs utilized as walls in makeshift shops, small tourist restaurants (decorated in cheap Thanksgiving decor year-round), large expanses of nothing except for the occasional hut, with people—families!—hanging up their laundry in the dry desert sun on clotheslines strung between non-functioning hulks of old trucks and refrigerators.

It's hard to put myself into that state of mind.

If I had *nothing* I could depend on, if food was hard to come by, and the only contact I had with the outside world was the fuzzy TV mounted on the wall in the corner of the one bar in town and what I could glean by staring at tourist buses driving past my shack, how would I see the world? How would I think it operated? What would be mysterious to me, and perhaps more importantly what would I have figured out that I don't know now, having lived the white, middle-class lifestyle?

I honestly don't know, and not knowing makes me sometimes question the validity of why I'm traveling to begin with.

If I can't ever truly know what it's like to grow up somewhere else—to be *from* these places—is it worth my time to try to understand the cultures? To try to put myself in their shoes as much as I'm able? Is it impossible to really understand other people in the empathetic way I would like?

In Buenos Aires, I didn't feel particularly distant from the local culture. True, there are many things in the *Porteño* culture I disagree with, but I understand why they feel this way and where the sentiments come from. I could walk down the street as a white guy with blue eyes and light hair (anything lighter than black there they call *rubio*, 'blonde'), knowing if I spoke decent Spanish with the correct accent, I would be treated as a local.

Who would know the difference? Metropolitan cities are like this. A melting pot as much as a salad bowl, where all kinds of mixing and matching goes on culturally and racially.

But outside of Buenos Aires, in other parts of Argentina, I'm acutely aware I'm different and reminded of it every time a local treats me like a tourist even before we speak. I look different, and that's enough to pick me out of the crowd.

Thai Tourism

This tendency to single out tourists was even more prominent a year and a half later when I found myself in Thailand.

A white guy walking down the street in even the smallest town in Thailand will find himself accosted by well-meaning tour guides, massage therapists, and food vendors. Everyone knows you're not from around there, so the chance you'll get a legitimate experience is quite small.

But this statement raises another question: is it possible to get a legitimate experience while traveling? And if so, what definition of 'legitimate' are we using?

It was Bangkok in particular that raised these questions for me. It's a city full of tourists and tourism, and the whole economy depends on making visitors feel welcome.

If that's the case, what could be more legitimate that embracing the tourist scene? Is my view of other countries skewed to the point where I expect to see tribal dances and handmade crafts everywhere I go? If I get 'gringo prices' on everything I buy, does that make my visit a less accurate portrayal of how things actually are in the country? Is the real problem that I'm frustrated to not be seeing the way things *were*?

It's tough to say, and I would imagine the answer (for me, at least) is somewhere in the middle of extreme possibilities.

On one hand, I have no idea what to expect when I move to a new country. The practice of allowing people to vote on where I live started because my ignorance about the world's cultures and countries is vast, and I figured other people (almost anyone, in fact) would have a better idea of where I should be spending my time than I would. This means my expectations are nearly nonexistent, and it's easy for locals to live up to very vague standards.

That being said, there is a huge Western bias (especially in the US) toward thinking all other countries should be more rugged, or at the very least have cultures incredibly different from our own.

If Paris were bulging with McDonald's and Walmarts instead of wine and baguettes, a lot of tourists would ask for their money back. Why would we even waste our time going to a place that looks like home, but is full of people we can't understand?

Now, I personally find language barriers to be excellent fun, and the differences in cultures (whatever they may be, and however subtle) to be an endless supply of fascination. But I am also mildly disappointed when I find myself in a place far from home geographically, but not *that* far from home culturally.

Lima, Peru was a good example of this; the Miraflores district in particular.

Mira-Frickin-Flores

I was in Miraflores for less than two weeks, and in that time I was able to explore the whole district and found very little that surprised me.

If I stepped out the front door of my hostel—I'm not making this up—directly in front of me was a Subway, a KFC, and a McDonald's. To the left, a Starbucks and a movie theater (showing only Hollywood flicks, in English with Spanish sub-titles), and around the corner was a Dunkin' Donuts. There was an alley of restaurants across the street, each bragging about their pizza and hamburgers. Everyone was drinking Coca-Cola.

Ah, the mysterious joys of travel.

But maybe this says something about how I travel, not travel in general.

Maybe my frustration at not being able to put my finger on how it would be to live in the places I go is the whole point? Maybe it's the *not* knowing that is inspiring. Maybe the places that leave my mind churning for answers are the right ones for what I hope to get out of the experience. Namely, unfamiliarity. Strangeness. Novelty.

When I'm handed something familiar, it's easy to fall into familiar routines. When I find myself in some completely foreign (no pun intended) circumstance, however, I have no habits to latch onto. I have to innovate and think hard. Figure out a way to make it work and imagine myself outside of my current or former lifestyle in order to find a solution.

Whatever biases I might have (and everyone has too many to count, no matter how much we try to be objective), maybe they are part of what makes travel worthwhile.

Without the baggage of where we come from and the biases inherent in our upbringing and life experiences, we wouldn't get stuck on bus rides from hell or caught in fistfights in foreign dance clubs or imagine wistfully what it might be like to live a completely different life, to see the world from a different angle.

Biased or not, I plan to continue trying to understand it all and to put myself in other peoples' shoes. Whether it improves the world or not, I feel pretty confident it improves me.

Chapter 3: Home for the First Time

The Surreality of Familiarity

My first return to the States after traveling through South America was shocking in its surreality.

I started by visiting my sister in Florida, which was where I left the country almost half a year before. I collapsed on the inflatable bed she provided and spent a few days adjusting to the humidity. My body would say things like "Wait, I thought we were in a desert? And why is all the food so sterilized?" To which I would reply "Shut up, body."

I blinked and I was in Los Angeles, hanging out with my ex-girlfriend and walking around a marina. We riled up some pelicans and made out on the docks. A mutual friend visited us at the hotel we were staying at and some drinks were quaffed, some cookies consumed.

There was a moment after a long, drunken conversation when the girls looked at each other and then at me, mischief in their eyes. They pulled me onto the bed with them, and it wasn't until afterward when we were all three lying around in our underwear, exhausted, that I stopped to think "Holy shit, this is my life."

My ex and I spent the rest of our week together walking along the beach, exploring the little town where we had decided to meet, occasionally gazing north up the coast, looking for *our* beach.

The pace, shockingly, wasn't hurried like we needed to fit in as much as possible. It was almost as if we had both come to terms with the fact that the relationship we had now was more stable and permanent than what we had before.

There was a connection and likely always would be. If the opportunity arose in the future, we'd get together again. We'd walk the beach and perhaps enjoy a week at a hotel in a small town. Cookies and third party involvement optional.

Another blink and I was in New York, visiting my friend Amber Rae who had recently moved from San Francisco to pursue her passions on the East Coast.

Her story caught the attention of a production company that wanted to create a TV show with her as the star, and she asked me to be in the pitch video.

Amber had a friend who lent her his fancy apartment on Union Square, and he gave his permission for me to crash there with her. It wasn't until later that I realized the Derek she kept referring to was actually Derek Sivers, the founder of CD Baby, a frequent TED speaker, and a bit of an entrepreneurial celebrity.

Amber and I explored some of the new, hip districts of New York, though 'hip' was a title that seemed to apply to different areas every time I visited the city. We had some amazing pizza and checked out the new exhibits at the museums (which are some of my favorites in the world). Photos were taken. Wine was consumed.

We attended a prom-themed party put on by the folks at Foursquare, held at a local public school. Partway through the bash, I half-drunkenly started talking to a half-drunk gal who did design work for the company. I don't remember which of us suggested we go make out in the bathroom, prom-style, but we ended up being classy and headed to a classroom down the hall instead.

During that trip I also had the opportunity to meet up with Seth Godin, one of my favorite authors and marketing-philosophers.

One of Amber's good friends knows Seth quite well and he set up a meeting in a connoisseur-style tea shop a double-handful of blocks away. We arrived 20 minutes early and walked in to find him typing away at his laptop in the corner (obviously a man who has mastered time-management to a degree we could only dream of).

We discussed Amber's TV project and Seth asked what I was up to. It was an amazing experience, and I walked away feeling that, yes, this guy is just as brilliant in real life as he is in writing. I sort of expected it to be otherwise.

On my way out of town, I received a response to the 'thank you' message I had emailed Derek. He said I was very welcome, and that he would love to meet me next time we were in the same hemisphere. A year later in Singapore, that meet up finally happened. Good conversations are worth waiting for.

On my way out of the US, plane tickets pointing me first toward Australia, then to New Zealand, I mentally acknowledged for the first time that my new lifestyle was a commitment I could keep, but that it would change *everything*.

It was hard to see the differences while living in Argentina and traveling through South America because everything was new. There was no familiar yardstick to measure what was bizarre and what was totally normal. Strange stuff happened, but I took it in as a traveler, which meant I was ready for anything.

Upon returning home, however, I found my country was still mostly the same, but I had changed.

I was much more mobile and felt more capable. I felt like the world was made up of a mad tangle of options, and all I had to do was pick which strand I wanted to follow and then weave my way along the path I chose until I saw one I liked better.

Old barriers seemed porous. New barriers seemed like a fun challenge.

I had no idea what to expect from my life, and it was the most liberating feeling I'd ever had. I checked my bag, walked down the boarding ramp and smiled as I sat down in the slightly claustrophobic seat that would carry me to Oceania.

My final thought as we took off was 'let's see where this strand goes.'

Catch and Release

Every once in a while I'll write about my relationships, though I tend to focus on the philosophy and ethics of the situation a lot more than the specifics.

The reasons behind this are twofold:

First, I don't want to bring attention to the women I date because they're generally talented, intelligent, ambitious women who will make or have made a name for themselves in other ways. It would be unfair of me to turn attention away from what they stand for and do, and turn them into 'that girl Colin dated' in the minds of some readers. I don't think most people intend to think in terms of relationship-labels, but it does happen and I owe it to them to prevent that.

Second, I don't want attention to be pulled away from the points I'm trying to make and to become embroiled in a discussion about my sex life, relationships, or anything else I consider to be less important in that context (this kind of gossip is incredibly over-publicized in the media: who's sleeping with whom seems to dominate the public's attention, even when there are far more important things to be talking about).

There is still quite a bit that can be gleaned from hearing about other people's experiences, though, so let's see how much I can divulge without falling into the 'poetry for loves long-lost' segment of writers.

The question I probably get asked the most regarding my lifestyle and relationships is "Don't you think you'll want to settle down at some point? Find one girl and have a family and a dog and a trampoline?"

The next most common question is "Are there really girls who would want to date someone they know, and who won't be sticking around more than a few months or weeks?"

The first question is a little easier to answer, believe it or not.

At this point in my life, no, I don't want those things, and the phrase 'settle down' explains perfectly why I would want to avoid such a situation.

Settling, to me, means you're no longer striving, reaching for the highest branch, and working hard to compete and achieve and aim your sights higher and higher. It means you'll take what's available, no more than an arm's-length away, and accept that this is the best you can do, the best you should want to do. Anything else, this phrase implies, would be flying too close to the sun, and you know what happens to people who do that.

Settling is one of the most frightening concepts I can think of.

I remember settling, back when I was a kid who tested well in school and didn't need to work too hard for anything. Life was easy, sure, but it was never great. I never felt incredible euphoria or extreme pain. Instead of reaching the peaks and valleys of the human experience, my capacity was limited to a small region right in the center.

Contentment, you might call it.

I picture this continuum as one of those machines they have in hospitals to monitor your heartbeat.

A healthy heart has high-highs and low-lows, and as long as you're living they keep going up and down, up and down. A dead person's heart, in contrast, has a line that goes right down the middle. To me, being content is like flatlining, with no life left in the body.

At the same time, I know the only constant in life is change and that my opinions about everything can be radically altered with one newly acquired bit of information or one novel and influential experience. My whole worldview could pivot in a snap, so for me to say it's impossible that my views on this subject will ever change would be naive.

As for the second question, I was asking myself this same thing when I started traveling. Exactly how tough will it be to find women I like who are also okay with a relationship that won't be forever; one that has a pre-set time limit?

I was worried about this because in a way, I wasn't even sure how *I* felt about it, much less women I hadn't even met yet from a culture I knew nothing about. "This could quickly become a very lonely lifestyle," I wrote to a friend in an email right after I left the US for Argentina.

But shockingly, girls have been willing to give it a shot. Many of them, actually. And rather than it being some kind of sacrifice, it turns out they take to the idea enthusiastically, as if the concept of time-limitations frees them from some socially induced responsibility they otherwise feel they must adhere to.

My expectation, before I started dating while traveling, was that the conversation would go something like this:

I would say:

"I'm so glad that we finally had a chance to grab a cup of coffee, and I think you're great and would love to see you again sometime. I want to make clear, though, that I'll be leaving in a few weeks and I don't do long-distance relationships. This would be a short-term thing, but there would be no pressure or expectations either way, so long as we both have a good time while we're together."

To which she would reply:

"You're a monster!" She'd then dump her hot coffee into my lap. An ambulance would be called, but they wouldn't be able to save my poor, burnt, man-parts.

The reality of the situation was something much more like this:

"I'm so glad that we finally had a chance to grab a cup of coffee, and I think you're great and would love to see you again sometime. I want to make clear, though, that I'll be leaving in a few weeks and I don't do long-distance relationships. This would be a short-term thing, but there would be no pressure or expectations either way, so long as we both have a good time while we're together."

The reply is then usually something akin to:

"Huh, this is way different from anything I've ever done before but I'm willing to give it a shot. I like you a lot, too, and if we can have a few good weeks together that will be worth it, even if it's not building toward something that lasts forever."

And her response is accurate, except for the last part.

Although we may not be building toward a romantic relationship that lasts forever, we *are* building the foundation of an incredibly strong friendship, and that does last forever, so long as both people continue to respect and care about each other.

That's not to say all attraction dies after we're divided by geography—I have had women come and visit me in other countries, and I've gone back to visit them as well—but the key difference between this kind of arrangement and just being 'fuck buddies' is that it's based on the premise that we're friends first, and anything on top of that is just an added bonus.

This approach works well with all first dates, actually. Sitting down for a cup of coffee is a lot less of a commitment than enjoying an alcoholic beverage together, because with one you're stimulating your brain and setting the scene for a good conversation, while the other comes laced with implicit sexuality and deadening the part of your brain which makes rational decisions.

If your first date is just a meeting between new friends with no expectations, then if the bottom falls out and you end up not taking things any further, or if you do and then pull back, ending the physical relationship, you at least have that friendship to fall back on and you haven't lost the core of what made your relationship strong to begin with.

I've spent a good deal of my life since my mid-teens trying to become a better person. To be someone I have an easier time respecting, but also the kind of person other people would want to be around, that other people like.

I wanted to be, you might say, a good catch. A guy any gal would be proud to bring home to their parents. I know now there are plenty of fish in the sea and that an important part of dating while traveling seems to be finding someone I'm into who approaches dating with the same catch and release policy that I do.

Me and My Brand Orbits

When I lived in Los Angeles, I ran a branding studio.

Now, from the road, I help people brand themselves and their businesses.

Part of why I'm able to do this is because I put my branding where my persona is. My brand sells my branding.

I'm going to tell you a bit about how I developed my personal brand. I'm not afraid of doing this, that you might steal my thunder, because a good brand is two things above all else:

(1) True. That is, it's an accurate representation of what it's presenting.

(2) Communicative. This means it will express things about you faster than most people's image will, and that's a good thing (unless your brand doesn't adhere to the first point, in which case you might want to focus on fixing that before you accidentally start communicating lies more clearly).

Like an idea for a business, the best brand is one you can talk about because no one else can steal it or build it as well as you. After all, if someone else is better at being you than you are, you've got much bigger issues to deal with than figuring out a personal brand.

My personal brand focuses on a few key points that should be apparent to a stranger stumbling upon my website, anyone meeting me in person, or anyone hearing about me or my work from a friend.

First, I'm a young, professional guy doing something non-traditional with his life.

What I'm doing is ostensibly something many people would like to be doing for a living, and it involves travel and personal development. Additionally, there's kind of a rock star quality to it all, with the impression there are lots of parties, drinks, and hobnobbing with remarkable, attractive people along the way.

Those are the primary takeaways, the things I make sure the non-verbal aspects of my brand convey. If you look at the photos of me around the net, the stories people tell and the interviews I do, you'll find most of them reinforce many or all of these primary branding points.

The secondary parts of my brand flesh things out a bit more, adding more depth to the storyline.

Things like my mobile lifestyle, and how I choose my new home based on the votes of perfect strangers. My writing may come up, or the fact that I'm always engaged in some kind of extreme lifestyle experiment. More information might surface about my current business endeavors (or the businesses I've run in the past), or that my background is in branding. A few specifics may follow ("He's lived in Thailand" or "He left a successful business in LA to pursue his dream of traveling"), but the overarching storyline is still left for the next round.

Finally, the tertiary bits are revealed to people who dig deeper looking for consistencies and story arcs in my writing, those who have listened to a lot of interviews I've done, or to people who have spoken to me personally and asked the right questions.

This is where the really juicy details come into play, like specifics about the breakup party my ex-girlfriend and I had, or the fact that she and I (and another blogger) went on a road trip across the US (and what hijinks ensued along the way). Stories about my geeky past or milestones completed in reaching my goal to travel while doing what I love. Rumors about trysts with other known personalities and debates about the totality of my personal philosophies also reside here (though the rumor-group is generally a different crowd than the philosophical-debaters).

Basically, a good brand has layers, like a Peanut Butter M&M.

The candy shell is great, and it had better be because most people won't make it past that stage unless they really enjoy it.

The chocolate filling is revealed to those who dig a little deeper, and those who want to know even more are rewarded with a peanut butter core *inside* the chocolate.

Each individual layer stands on its own, but the whole package is the most appetizing of all. You have to work to present aspects of your life in an order that makes sense, and doesn't give everything away from the get-go. That's usually the hardest part.

Too often I see people with amazing stories exposing everything in the first cluttered paragraph or interview. This is really too bad, because people just looking for the basics about you respond to a biographical scrapheap the same way they'd respond to a grenade hurled through the window of their car. It's not at all welcome and just too much to take in all at once.

To use journalistic terminology, you need a headline, a hook, and then a lead before you can get people to read the article. A catchy headline will get people to come visit, the hook will keep them long enough to hit them with the key thesis of the story, and then the story, if well-written, will keep them reading the rest of the paper (or I guess, for the sake of this metaphor, it gets them reading other articles you've written and will write).

Something most people don't seem to realize about building a personal brand is that really good ones evolve over time.

You may have a favorite book you enjoy reading over and over, but wouldn't it be even cooler if that same book was longer and had a different (but equally satisfying) ending each time you read it?

That's the idea here. If you don't show growth, your most loyal readers/followers/subscribers/customers/clients won't have any reason to stick around. If you aren't growing, neither are they.

This means that as you change as a person, you should implement changes across your brand. Evolve each layer and you'll find you're able to reach completely different audiences.

I'll give you an example from the evolution of my brand.

When I first start blogging at Exile Lifestyle, I did so as a design studio owner who had found success segueing into branding. That success led me to change the way I ran my business so I would be able to travel the world while working.

I talked about personal development, emphasized 'lifestyle design'-style formulas and philosophies, and explained the process of stripping down a rooted-life and making it more mobile.

Over time, though, I became less focused on design-business topics. I also stopped giving so much straight-up advice and started telling more stories and asking more questions.

I had moved past wanting to give step-by-step instructions on how to become more efficient or become location independent (other people were doing this, and probably much better than I could) and I was spending more time taking in new experiences and figuring out how to live more in-line with my core beliefs. I started to weave more tales that entertained while also exploring my personal philosophies.

As you can imagine, this pivot changed the makeup of my casual reader audience quite a bit. The folks who wanted a younger Tim Ferriss moved on to some of the more Tim Ferriss-like personalities out there, and I attracted more travelers, philosophers, and vicarious-experiencers to my outer orbit.

The inner-two rings, however, tend to retain their numbers while adding a new collection of people to the mix each time the outer ring changes. This is desirable, as these are the people who really make up the core of your audience anyway. They're the ones who define the personality of your community. They're the ones you want to fight hard to keep around.

This is not to say that the outer ring of transient readers is worthless or shouldn't be paid attention to. They're just much more finicky and more likely to move on at the drop of a hat. You can't make important life decisions based on the habits of people who always have one foot out the door.

Outer-orbit people are like customers who shop at your store only because they clipped your coupons that week. Next week, they'll head to wherever the best coupons are coming from. Nothing wrong with it, but hard to plan for, and you shouldn't kill yourself trying provide the best coupons for them while your loyal customers are ignored.

Your business will have similar rings of customers. You as a person will have similar groups of friends that orbit around you at difference distances.

This is just one way of thinking about how you present yourself, but it's the method I've found to be most resilient over time, and most helpful in figuring out how to quickly and accurately get my message across to as many people as possible.

Just don't try to copy my brand. I guarantee I'm a better Colin Wright than you.

Chapter 4: Plotting the Island Lifestyle

A Stressful Sense of Non-Danger

I don't think I've ever been more jumpy than when I was living in Christchurch, New Zealand, a place where the most dangerous things roaming the countryside are jovial, drunken Kiwis.

What you have to understand is that I had just come from a tour through South America, and before that I was living in Argentina for four months.

While I was living in Buenos Aires, I had to throw a (weak, awkward) punch to defend myself against a pair of muggers. My fighting back stunned them long enough for me to escape. But what if it hadn't? What if?

I saw another man get mugged while in Buenos Aires. He was middle-aged, slightly overweight and wearing a tweed jacket. He was walking toward me on the other side of the street about a block away when a couple of teenagers ran up behind him, punched him in the stomach, pushed him against the wall, and held a knife against his throat while they went through his pockets.

In seconds they were off around the corner, and by the time the man regained his senses and started yelling '*Ayudame! Ayudame!*' ('Help me! Help me!'), they were long gone.

The combination of witnessed muggings, my own feather-weight bout mentioned before, and the first-hand stories of people involved with black markets and bribery rings throughout South America meant my trip prior to arriving in Christchurch was punctuated by run-ins with corruption, gang violence, criminal activity, and in one case getting punched in the face at a gay dance club in Lima by a jealous boyfriend.

As a result of these extracurricular activities (and those required just to stay alive), my adrenaline had been permanently turned up to 11. When I finally arrived in Christchurch, I was a mess.

Picture this:

I would be walking down the street at about 1am, making my way back home after a night of drinking hard cider with a jolly clutch of Kiwis, and I'd stop at the entryway of a flat, open, park, which was the shortest way home.

I'd take a moment and assess the situation. In the middle of a sidewalk that traced its way through the park, there was a statue, which commemorated some noble personage or another by perching him atop a horse and chiseling him into granite for future generations to wonder about. Was someone hiding behind it? There were lights all over the place, but no homes nearby. Would anyone hear me if I yelled for help? Shadows from the trees were the perfect size for hiding behind.

But in the end I would force myself to walk through the park because I knew in the rational part of my brain that crime simply wasn't a problem in New Zealand the way it was in my previous home country. People were still talking about a robbery that happened two months before I arrived! The chance of my becoming a statistic in Christchurch was incredibly low. I would be more likely to get hit on the head with a meteorite.

This didn't stop my spider-sense from tingling, though. And tingle it did, all throughout my time in New Zealand, through my road trip across the United States, and up until the end of my four months in Thailand.

There was a moment during one of the last weeks in Bangkok when I was walking home with a girl I had been seeing, and I couldn't shake the feeling we were being followed.

She and I were having a lovely conversation after a great night out, but my mood darkened when I caught scuffling sounds nearly out of earshot. I felt the hairs on the back of my neck rise up, as if I was being watched. My date picked up on my internal alarm, noticing how I glared into every alley and checked our reflection in every street window to see if we were being followed. Eventually she said "What's going on with you?"

I paused, realized what I had been doing and told her about my South American reflex for bad-situation detection.

We stopped walking for a moment and I verbally acknowledged everything I was keeping track of, and one by one I realized the shadows or sounds or alleyways that I was paying such close attention to were harmless. My associations were clearly out of whack.

Thankfully, being called out on it and going through the list of possible dangers out loud (and being wrong on each count) helped quite a bit, and the wary sensations haven't been as strong lately. I'm still careful, but not to a paranoid degree.

However, I'm still concerned about meteorites. Have you seen the statistics on those things?

A Serious Disconnect

The smells are familiar, the colors are familiar, and the soft buzz of conversation from across the room is the icing on the cake. I close my eyes and I'm transported to every Starbucks I've ever visited anywhere in the world.

Remarkable brand consistency.

Except there's something very different about this particular Starbucks. At this location, nestled among clothing stores and skate shops in downtown Christchurch, my computer informs me there's no free WiFi. I open up the browser to see what's what and discover a landing page asking for money.

And it's not cheap. This greedy little browser window is demanding megabucks for megabytes, and with a very constricting cap on data, to boot. There's no way I'll be able to do any work here.

I pack up my laptop and finish the remainder of the overpriced drink I purchased for the occasion and resign myself to the simple truth: there's no fast, affordable Internet in New Zealand.

This truth is immediately followed by the shadow of another that's more question than statement: this means I hate New Zealand, right?

Some countries have, in the past few years, decreed high-speed Internet access to be a basic human right.

If you look at places like Finland and Estonia, you'll see their governments are taking connectivity so seriously that they've worked the net into their citizens' benefits package. Just for living in these countries, people have a *right* to Internet access. It's a nice thought, isn't it? Especially at times like this, when simple pleasures like checking Facebook or watching cats sleep (cutely) on YouTube seem so far out of reach.

Leaving the aromas and chit-chat of Starbucks behind, I meander down the sidewalk, peeking into other coffee shops and tiny bookstores I pass, looking for the telltale 'Free Wifi' sign in a window or door, but I come up short.

There are Internet access points galore, of course, but each and every one has an ambitious fee attached, and is clearly not intended for anyone looking to do more than send a few emails. Without attachments.

Caps are set on the amount of data you can access before your money is used up, and 256MB seems to be the standard. Thankfully, the speeds are so low you'd be lucky to download a large image in a reasonable amount of time, much less something like a video, so chances are you won't be able to use the whole 256MB in the hour you're allotted anyway.

Savages.

I curse the situation internally, thinking how the next time I'm able to access the net for any amount of time, I'm going to whine and complain and make others feel my pain. This travesty shall be tweeted!

Until then, I try to hold back the helpless rage and tell myself that it's not New Zealand's fault that things are this way. It's Australia's.

Well, that's not really fair either, but kind of.

New Zealand is woefully underserved when it comes to Internet because the 'pipeline' of information (an undersea cable) between the US and New Zealand goes first through

Australia and then scatters out to the smaller islands nearby. In essence, little NZ gets Australia's Internet backwash, and there's only so much of it to go around.

Believe it or not, before the early 2000's when this Southern Cross cable was connected and turned on, prices were even higher and speeds even lower. I shudder at the thought, as memories of my childhood dial-up days buzz sadistically in the recesses of my mind. Never again!

Defeated, I head back to my apartment hoping there will be a WiFi signal to catch as it drifts lazily through the breeze toward my window. I suspend disbelief for a few seconds before acknowledging to myself that there won't be one. I've tried every corner of that place, including the balcony and lounge areas upstairs, and there's not so much as a whisper of a promise of a signal anywhere.

Arriving home, I slump down on the couch and think about how sad it is that I'm a block away from a college where people are somehow learning without reliable wireless Internet access. It's a travesty (and a little impressive, in the same way that cuneiform is impressive).

I've been in this situation a few times before, though, and I know that the solution to my problem is also the issue: the Internet has become, above all else, my connection to the world.

While on the road you can put down roots, but they can never go too deep. In four months time you can build some strong friendships, but when you leave, you leave little behind and take even less with you.

You have memories, but everything else is online. The photos, the conversations, the connections to the people you miss are all gone in flash if you can't find an access ramp to the information superhighway.

If life is a University, the Internet is my Quad. It's where I meet up with friends for lunch and find out what's going on with their relationships, professional lives, and families.

Being cut off from the Internet is like being cut off from the world. It's suddenly losing touch with everything that's going on elsewhere, and all the people who are making those things happen.

It's a feeling that's hard to describe to someone who has never felt the online-omnipresence that comes with net-fluency; the feeling that you can make anything happen, make things better, more beautiful, or even just more entertaining.

As in real life, you have a reputation to uphold and assets to build online, all of them cobbled together from pixels rather than atoms.

Losing access to that part of your life is like losing access to air. You know that you can survive without it for a little while, but you've also become quite fond of having it around, and you don't realize its full value until it's gone.

Above all else though, the Internet, to me, is consistency.

Though I may change my location, profession, dietary habits, style of dress, or anything else about myself at the drop of a hat, I know that online, I have a home.

There are safe-houses I've built for myself on the web, and nestled amidst the tangle of bits and bytes I have a mailbox which anyone can find at any time, even when I'm not around. That doesn't change, even when everything else does. People can find me and I can find them. It's a nice feeling.

It's a little like people who become more conservative about some aspect of their life when something tragic happens; say, they become more religious after a family member dies, even though they seldom attended services before.

That service, that routine and tradition, suddenly becomes very important because the whole world has shifted overnight and everyone needs something solid and unchanging to hold onto when everything else seems to be upended. Stability is necessary, even for those who thrive on change.

And so I sit here on my black leather couch, staring blankly at a television set I will never turn on (a technological remnant from the days before the Internet), feet propped up on the coffee table, wondering with no hint of irony what people do when they don't have news to read, conversations to participate in, or emails to answer.

I tilt my head back, lay it on the couch and rest my hands on my thighs.

I pick a point on the ceiling. Yes, that one will do. Focus, unfocus. Staring. Hmmm.

Disconnecting is hard.

Scared Sober

There are two twenty-something Kiwi dudes goofing off while driving along a back road. They're clearly drunk.

The driver swerves and flies off the road into a ditch and plows into a tree. You can hear the deafening sound of glass shattering and metal crunching. Their surprised screams are cut short.

A little while later, the passenger of the destroyed car regains consciousness, and though horrified at what's happened, he's thrilled to be alive. He looks up at the driver (who, due to how the car landed, is above him) and realizes his friend is dead and hanging from his seatbelt. A horrible silence fills the car.

Moments pass as the passenger realizes he can't escape the car. His dead friend is held, marionette-like, above him, his eyes wide open. The passenger shrinks back in terror and then screams 'WHAT?! WHAT DO YOU WANT? STOP LOOKING AT ME!'

The corpse falls onto the drunk, still-living Kiwi and crazed screaming fills the air as the screen fades to black. Words appear and are read by a disembodied voice: "If you drink then drive, you're a bloody idiot."

New Zealand TV is interesting, especially the news, because as a nation they generally have little of the rampant crime and violence a lot of other countries suffer from, so they tend to obsess over other things, like drunk driving.

And *obsessed* is putting it mildly. I've never seen so many puff pieces during prime time, and I come from the land of 24-hour news networks scrambling to find material to fill time between ad-breaks. It's a luxury, really, when there's so little crime, drugs, and the like that a country can afford to have yet another story about sheep-sheering headlining the news at seven.

But despite the small number of serious problems in New Zealand, you would think it was the most dangerous place in the world based on their Public Service Announcements.

I've seen a lot of PSAs during my travels, but New Zealand takes the cake for having some of the most disturbing. Even more disturbing (in a way) are the somewhat-mundane and everyday topics into which they instill fear.

There's one that features a mother who is pulled away from her cooking for a moment to see what her child is up to.

Next frame, the house is on the fire, the woman and her child are shrieking in terror.

Final scene, the house has become a charred ruin, along with all of their possessions, hopes, and dreams.

The message? Don't leave your cooking unattended, or your house will burn to the ground.

PSAs like this make me wonder just how many Kiwi houses have been burnt-down due to unattended cooking. Two? Ten? How many cooking fires would warrant a well-produced and shockingly horrific public service announcement? That's a big expense for what I would imagine is a somewhat small problem.

And if that isn't New Zealand, I don't know what is.

This is a country that has it pretty good, and aside from the tragic earthquake in Christchurch that essentially knocked down the city in 2011, the people there live really pleasant lives. The Kiwi culture is friendly and welcoming. The landscape is gorgeous on a scale I've never imagined possible, and there are no local animals that see human beings as prey. Hell, even their alcohol is good. In fact, eating and drinking well is part of the culture.

But according to the PSAs, that same high-quality alcohol is part of the problem.

The most recent PSA to make global headlines starts with a man swinging his child around in the backyard, holding onto one leg and one arm. The kid is having fun, and everyone is laughing and having a good time.

Then the man drinks. And drinks. And drinks some more.

Later that night, the neighborhood party is still going on, but this man is *very* drunk, and he picks up his kid like he did before and swings him around once again, but this time he's in the living room and slams the child's head into the side of the entertainment center. Crunch.

Suddenly, everyone panics, running to help the critically injured kid while the man's wife yells at him to leave, go, just go. The implication is that his drinking ruined the night *again*. This is a common theme in these types of commercials in New Zealand.

Every culture has demons. Every country is rife with different concerns, and these worries are generally vented through popular media like TV, billboards, and full-page newspaper ads.

There are signs up around Thailand reminding locals to smile at foreigners, which helps keep their tourism industry churning along, but makes real relationships between the two groups difficult.

Look at any commercial or TV show in Bangkok and you'll find the hero is whiter than the rest of the characters, and walk into the grocery store and you'll be hard-pressed to find lotions that don't say 'Whitening!' on the label.

In the States, media messages generally revolve around what we need to consume in order to achieve the lifestyle we desire.

There are also well-meaning ads intended to keep people off drugs and to avoid driving drunk, but most of these are easily overshadowed by the enormous billboards and sensational TV spots featuring sexy people wearing designer labels who are drinking and driving nice cars.

Each culture has a million stories to tell; stories that eventually become part of the cultures themselves. The stories that are given the most prominence—because of who is telling them, where they appear, or how well they are told—tend to shape the direction of the people, and largely determine what the next chapter in the story will be.

Places like New Zealand are working hard to fight the death- and injury-by-alcohol problem that has become *baked* into their culture, and to do this they tell the story in a different way: if you drink and drive, you're a bloody idiot. Simple as that.

In Thailand, the story is something else: people with whiter skin live better lives and have more fun. Let's all get paler! Such is the path to fulfillment; and this storyline will likely continue unabated for some time.

Similarly, in the US we're told if we can just get our hands on the right stuff, hang out with the right crowd, and be seen at the right places we will be complete.

The trouble with stories is that often that's all they are.

There is rampant discontent amongst upper-middle-class Americans who have found themselves with everything they're told they should want, and yet they somehow remain unhappy.

It's a never-ending cycle and a self-perpetuating one. Maslow's Hierarchy of Needs isn't a pyramid, it's a perspective drawing. The apex can never be reached. It will be just a little bit longer, we're told—work a little harder and paradise will be on the other side of this next hill, or the next one, or the next one—and it's easy to see why a deadly breed of frustration could emerge after finding ourselves lied to over and over again in this way.

But that's how this kind of story works. It doesn't end, it just evolves.

If the Kiwis cut down on the drinking problem, some new issue will rear its head and take its place (perhaps the unattended cooking fires that are supposedly ravaging the nation?).

There will always be a next step, and regardless of what common sense or pop culture tells us, there's not going to be a point where we can put down our laptops, turn off our brains and say 'Whew, done. Time to go do nothing, completely philosophically fulfilled.'

Every finish line is a horizon, not an ending.

Chai-Diving

Jack and Jennifer have just broken up.

Jack is coping with this the way I imagine he probably copes with many of life's difficulties: he's left on a road trip.

My older sister Katherine is sitting up front, and I'm in the back seat watching Mount Cook shrink smaller and smaller on the horizon as we pass an enormous glacial lake. Its water is the color of some obscure precious stone no one but precious stone enthusiasts have heard of. It's some kind of blue, but kind of green, but not turquoise. Not teal. It's glacial-water colored.

We cross a bridge, one of the many single-lane bridges we've come across on the road trip thus far, and pull over to the side of the road near a rest stop overlooking the lake.

There are cairns (piles of stones, stacked as landmarks for travelers or as an exercise in Zen-like patience) littering the area, and it's a testament to the low-degree of rabble-rousing in New Zealand that someone hasn't come along and kicked them all over.

This country! Land of cairns!

In the US, someone would have stomped them like so many sand castles, or covered them in glue and taken them home. With or without guards, something this tenuous wouldn't have survived where I come from. But here the only guards are a few birds, and they don't look very tough.

We hop back in the car—a beat-up sedan of unmemorable make, model, or color—and turn back on the radio, which almost picks up stations but always at the periphery of listenable-range. A little less static and it would be just fine, a little more static and it would be easier to call it 'just noise' and turn it off.

Our ears wade through audible-limbo for the next five hours that it takes to get to Queenstown, at the southern tip of the South Island of this southern country.

When we arrive, it's dark and rainy. We're able to find a few beds in a hostel, but only just. The people at the front desk are friendly, but it's clear they're ready to hit the sack and our late arrival has pushed back their plans.

We're all stationed in different eight-bed rooms, and as I say goodnight to Jack and my sister, I walk into my darkened dorm, unsure whether there are actual people in each of the beds. I pull out a tiny flashlight I keep in my bag (acutely aware of how loud the velcro sounds as I open it) and see the bed closest to the door is free. I undress and pass out to the sound of the rain and the proximity-chill from the window a foot from my head.

The next morning, Jack and Katherine are ready to go. They're chattering about bungee jumping and they want to hit some white water rafting as well.

As the self-proclaimed adventure-sport capital of the world, Queenstown is happy to oblige, and the folks at the registration desk of the hostel set them up with a package deal that includes both of these adrenaline-pumping-undertakings for a lower-than-normal price.

I head into town with them, walking through the rain to grab a hot drink before heading out; but at the last second I say, "So guys..."

I decide not to go.

Maybe it's the chai latte, so wonderfully warm in contrast to the cold, stinging rain still falling outside. Maybe it's the continuous proximity to people, having had my sister stay with me for the past week, and the lack of personal space that's making me crave time alone. Maybe it's because I've got work to do and I haven't been able to answer the zillion emails piling up in my inbox.

Or maybe I just don't want to. Not today.

Ever since I started Exile Lifestyle, people seem to think I'm some kind of adventure junkie. Like a day isn't worth getting up for unless there's a cobra to wrestle or a shark-filled ocean to swim across. I'm doing something a little crazy and experimental and untested, therefore I probably get my rocks off by seeking out thrills and facing death at every turn.

Honestly, though, that kind of adventure doesn't really do much for me.

Sure, I love trying new things, and I love taking risks. But roller coasters have never really gotten my heart pumping, and the adult versions of roller coasters, like bungee jumping and white water rafting, don't either.

Sometimes I'll take part and the adventure ends up being kind of fun, but is it worth the money and time it takes to prepare, for me? Not really.

I went skydiving after being double-dog dared by a friend and it was a good time, but do I feel the need to do it again? No. Would I have done it without someone pressuring me? Probably not. I'd much rather spend my time risking my livelihood or challenging cultural mores than jumping off something really, really high.

So today I sit and write, sipping my chai latte and watching the rain, and for now this, *this* is what makes me feel alive. No matter what others may think or want of me, the risks that I enjoy the most are ones that allow me to enjoy the simple pleasures in life when I'm able.

Chai-diving. Some days, I prefer chai-diving.

Imperfect Moments

We met in an imperfect way.

Online. We met online.

Though technically we met in person first, because you can't *literally* meet someone online. Not yet. Someday we'll have the technology, but right now we're stuck with digital impressions: optimized photos from just the right angle and clever conversation, both carefully edited to remove anything incriminating or unflattering.

But we first communicated online. And I was the reason we didn't meet up sooner.

I was busy and exhausted from a month of travel and not terribly optimistic I would meet someone I really clicked with on the dating site I joined when I arrived in Christchurch.

I could tell that in New Zealand online dating was still very much a weird thing—what, you can't get a date in real life?—and the range of dating site options reflected this bias. They were pretty second-rate properties.

The first concern with this gal was her photo. There wasn't one.

I find it increasingly difficult to trust people who don't have photos attached to their profile on dating sites, social networks, or even their blogs. What are they hiding, exactly? Why won't they let me get close to them so I can understand where their ideas are coming from? Why won't they let me analyze their bias to improve my interpretation of their words? And why can't I see if they're hot?

Clearly, the cards were stacked against us from the get-go.

I remember telling her I wouldn't be able to get together for coffee as we had planned because I was asked to give a talk to a group of young professionals. I would be busy putting the talk together for the next several days. Sorry, bad timing.

Additionally, after the presentation I would be heading up north to take in the hot springs of Hamner and the beautiful landscapes of Nelson, along with all the fabulous tree/mountain/lake-strewn wilderness in between. Not really time to grab a drink.

But it turns out New Zealand is a small country, and Christchurch an even smaller city. She shot me a message the day before my presentation saying she had just received an invitation from a friend to come see Colin Wright speak to the Canterbury Young Professionals, and she put two and two together.

She would be there in the audience and would introduce herself afterward.

No pressure.

Let me tell you from experience, the only thing stranger than a blind date is a blind meeting in which you're giving a presentation to dozens of people and the other person you're supposed to meet is somewhere in the audience. Watching. Judging. Knowing who you are while they remain incognito. It's the perfect storm of discomfort.

I made it through the talk, though, and afterward she introduced herself and we chatted for a bit. During this quick back-and-forth (which was frequently interrupted by other people who had watched the talk and wanted to stay in touch or get a bit of advice), two things became clear:

First, she was an interesting woman and I could see having some long conversations with her over a cup of coffee or something stronger.

Second, she was very cute. I immediately thought 'why the hell wouldn't *you* put a picture up on a dating site?'

Actually, I was pretty sure I already knew the answer to that question.

I've learned over the years that, although guys can have a great deal of success dating online if they aren't total creepsters and have something interesting going on in their lives, girls usually receive a lot of messages, and generally from total sleezeballs who give the male gender a bad name.

So for girls, the best way to keep your spam down to a few dozen emails a day (instead of hundreds) is to stay off the 'pretty girls I want to nail' list these guys seem to pass amongst themselves. Hence, no pictures.

It's a sad but true fact that bad experiences with guys like this are what keep a lot of really top-notch women away from dating sites. There's only so much abuse a person can take, so they leave. Unfortunately, then the non-creepy guys who are looking for that type of girl also leave, and the cycle continues.

But every once in a while you find a real catch, and this girl—named Annabelle—seemed to be one of the good ones. I asked her if she would still be down to grab a cup of coffee with me before I leave, how about tomorrow? She accepted.

What happened the next few days is kind of a whirlwind because I was in the process of moving out of my apartment, saying goodbye to friends (though I would be returning briefly before leaving for the North Island, where I would be spending my remaining month in New Zealand), and heavily involved in being totally drenched by rain the whole time.

Annabelle was a warm presence in a cold (literally and figuratively) moment. She picked me up from my apartment as I was moving out and insisted I come stay with her instead of spending my final few days in Christchurch at a hostel.

We had a good thing for a fraction of a week, before I had to make my way up North. The relationship was intense, intellectual, sexual, a bit whimsical, fun—but it was also imperfect. Annabelle had some demons that I noticed right away, and I knew she saw mine as well.

It didn't matter, though, because we knew the most imperfect thing about our mini-relationship was that it came with a time-limit. It would end, and this allowed us to focus on enjoying the good and ignoring the bad. There was no time for drama, frustration, or sadness. Even a few hours of anything less than amazing would cost us a significant portion of our total time together, and we had come to an unspoken agreement that wasting any of that time would be unacceptable.

I returned from the North a week later, and I have bittersweet memories of how we spent our final few days together until I left Christchurch for good.

I remember the walk we took to the cafe and what we ate for breakfast. Snapshots of her waifish smile and bright, intelligent eyes looking at me from across the table are tucked away in my mental photo album, which I open up for perusal during sad, lonely moments on the road.

I still get warm-fuzzies from something she did the morning she dropped me off at the bus stop where I waited for the shuttle that would take me North to Hamner.

I had commented before how much I loved sushi, and though we tried to go out and get some several nights in a row, each time something came up and we weren't able to do so.

On our way into downtown Christchurch, she pulled over and said she needed to run a quick errand, and when she came back she had two plastic containers full of sushi that she had pre-ordered and bought for us to share on our last morning together.

There's a feeling that develops after you travel for a while, that no matter what the people around you say or how nicely they treat you, you just know eventually your presence there and anything you do will be forgotten. You're just a blip on the radar that will disappear forever as soon as you're gone. Their routines will resume, and as a transient, you were never *really* part of their reality.

But every once in a while someone does something that pulls you out of that morose reverie, and when it happens, you remember them fondly.

A stranger who insists on showing you around and invites you to dinner with their family, even though you can hardly communicate because of the language barrier.

A friend who continues to email you years after you last saw them and who tells you your visit changed their life for the better.

A woman you briefly date, who will likely move on quickly once you leave (and has every reason to do so), surprises you with a meaningful final gift, making it clear your being there meant something to her. Just like her being there meant something to you.

Over time, bad stuff fades. Eventually you'll forget the feelings associated with the horrible moments in your life and they will become just another story in your memoir.

The good moments, though—even the imperfect ones—tend to stick around forever.

Surprise sushi, waifish grins, and warm-fuzzies; the imperfect pleasures of travel.

06.17.2010 — Airport, Auckland, New Zealand

Probably the most difficult thing about traveling regularly is the numbness.

Oh, like anything else, you get used to it. You move your legs periodically so that they retain their senses. Over time you learn the best position for your other body parts, avoiding the painful blips of agony that pop up in your head, neck, arms, and shoulders after several hours on a bumpy bus or after a much-needed plane-nap.

Though physical numbness can be a bitch, there's also the numbness that comes with each and every new relationship you form. You *know* for a fact you'll be leaving in a matter of months at best, hours or minutes at worst, so there's an understood distance, at least from your end, between you and your family, friends, and those who are more than friends. The desire to build something strong is still there, but the ability to do anything about it—to solidify those friendships through persistent and consistent actions—isn't. You may *want* nothing more than to hold up your end of an interpersonal bargain, but it's simply not in the cards.

This is actually good for me in a way, as I'm beginning to suspect my ideal relationships may all have a time limit to begin with.

In all likelihood, I shouldn't even write about this, as it's really just a figment of a figment of a thought at the moment. Something I've barely noticed. But have identified it as a correlation, if not a causation.

I'm sitting here in the Auckland airport, waiting for a plane that won't take off for another four hours (it's 3am and I've been sitting here for four hours already) and I can't help but be a little introspective on my way out of the country.

It seems funny to me that I end up writing about this after meeting and staying with Annabelle on my way out of Christchurch. I really fell for her in the way that you fall for someone who surprises you with their awesomeness right before you're about to be separated from them by hundreds of miles of ocean and over a dozen time zones.

In a way it's good, I suppose, and I knew it would happen eventually.

It stands to reason there will be a lot of great people out there, and it further stands to reason I'll be attracted to a goodly number of them both physically and mentally. Doing what I'm doing, it only makes sense that sometimes I'll come across said people right before I leave. So maybe it's best that I get the first of such experiences out of the way early. That way I'll know I can move past the melancholy and instead remember the time we *did* have together for what it was.

Numbness will happen from time to time when you travel long term, and now that I've identified a new kind, it's time to figure out how to deal with it.

Feeling is returning. I'm preparing myself for the pins and needles.

Chapter 5: Cruisin' USA

Road Tripping

The Punch Line

It all started with a joke.

Well, it was a joke to everyone else. I have this habit of pursuing jokes that I think are actually good ideas, even when they're a little too 'out there' to succeed.

My theory is that often people will make dramatic proposals and then turn them into jokes because they don't think they're possible or likely. Doing so is a lot easier than moving forward with the difficult proposition and possibly failing.

To me, though, failure is an old friend. I also know it's the harbinger of impending success. So I seek out opportunities to potentially fail as they will either result in a much-wiser me or in some kind of fantastical victory that people talk about over dinner as one of those crazy things going on in the world.

To make the situation even more meta, the joke was posted as a comment on a blog belonging to a woman named Ash, and it was quipped by another named Andi.

Ash was an online friend I had somehow managed to never even Skype with in the year or so I'd known her through our blogging, and Andi was my ex-girlfriend.

I don't remember the exact conversation that took place in the comments that day and via email and instant message the next several weeks, so I'm going to make up something fictional but fairly-close-to-accurate:

Andi (to Ash): Dude, you and me. Road trip. Drunkenness and lipstick.

Ash (to Andi): Fuck yeah lady, we're doing this. Woo!

Colin: Guys, I want in on this. And let's get sponsors so we don't go broke doing it.

Ash and Andi (shouted): And how!

And so it was.

Making Out at Matsuri

A few months later, I was sipping drinks in a bar called Matsuri and looking at the custom menu they made up for the event. In my hand was a drink called 'The Exile' and though it was named for me, it wasn't my favorite of the bunch. Ginger and alcohol? Questionable choice. Everything else was fantastic, though, and people were starting to trickle in after a half hour of the 'will anybody show?' jitters.

I hate that feeling after you plan and set up a party, when, despite numerous RSVPs you still have no idea if anyone is actually going to show up. Perhaps I'm over-sensitive about this after a very awkward childhood where no one called me 'cool' (even jokingly) until my last year of college (except my mother: thanks Mom!).

It's a strange feeling, sending out invites, because essentially you're asking people to trust you when you say it will be a good time with good people in attendance. Of course, in order to get most people to show up, they have to know other people will already be there (most folks avoid being first to the party like they avoid diseased rodents), so it's a bit of a chicken/egg problem in a lot of cases.

But a few early arrivals made the wait at this party tolerable. An enthusiastic and friendly copywriter drove in from Washington D.C, an old classmate I knew from my design program in college decided to come, and a friend of Andi's who happened to be in town for business made it as well. We chatted, ordered drinks, and formed the nucleus of what would become our WBSQ (Way Below Status Quo) launch party. The name originated from a networking group Andi and I formed over a year before while living in Los Angeles, and it upheld our tradition of party-excellence. An hour later, the place was humming.

To my left, Andi's friend Kristin—a professional model who we had convinced the night before to buy a plane ticket to China on a whim—was chatting up Ash's drummer friend who was in town from Philadelphia for the event, along with an NYC-local named Kyle, who works at a think-tank full of technologists and philosophers.

To my right, a guy named Matthew, who sits in Union Square several days a week with a table, two chairs and a sign that says 'Creative approaches to what you've been thinking about,' was hobnobbing with Tony, an entrepreneur and owner of a popular co-working space in Manhattan who had recently been on the cover of Inc. Magazine. A skinny producer with an ironic handlebar mustache listened in, nodding his agreement periodically.

I was a little tipsy when I walked over to where Andi and Ash were standing and said "Well we're finally here, and this is going to be insane."

"YEAH!" yelled Andi. "Take your pants off!" She then smooched Ash and I on the cheek, which led to one big friendly smooching-session, followed by a series of photos in the men's bathroom (which included a whole lot of leg) in front of a painting portraying two rotund geisha going at it on the wall.

"Tomorrow is going to be rough," I said, though I don't think anyone was listening at that point.

We moved the party to another bar, then another. I made out with—I don't know, *someone*—in a photo booth. At around 4am, the gals, Tony, and I grabbed some pizza and tried to sober up. It didn't work.

Over the next few days, we met up with a series of young, ambitious personalities. Some were new comrades, like Arielle, an up-and-coming model-turned-entrepreneur I had been chatting with online for a few months, while others were old friends, like Amber Rae. We also attended the NYC Gay Pride Parade, despite the scorching heat.

A few mornings later, after spending several nights crashing with some friends of Andi's and a programmer (and great guy) named Dan who was kind enough to take us in until we left, Ash pulled up in her tiny Scion sedan and we crammed our bags into the trunk and fourth seat. Only slightly hungover from a 4th of July party the night before, we set off for the first leg of our journey up the East Coast toward Maine, a journey that would ultimately take us zig-zagging all across the United States.

Randall's Cape

About halfway through the road trip, we arrived in the Midwest. Having spent the better part of a year traveling full-time, I felt there was no way I would be surprised by my own country. Holy hell was I wrong.

The thing about the US is that each state is kind of like a different country. Actually, each community within each state could be its own country, they're all so different from one another. Each one is like a colorful collage of rival personalities and influences from all over the world that settled down and planted roots, and sometimes in the strangest places.

Because of this, a lot of the situations we came across were not exactly what we had expected. To illustrate this, let me tell you a little story about Randall and Cape Girardeau, Missouri.

Between New Orleans and Columbia, Missouri (where my family lives, and where we had planned to stay a few days at the road trip's halfway point), we were torn on where to stop for the night. We could head straight to Columbia, but it would be more fun to meet another cast of characters from another city beforehand, adding a new batch of real life friends to our network.

The obvious choice would be St. Louis, a place where I had a few friends from college, and the second-largest city in the state. We were bound to have some readers who would come out and have some drinks with us there. I also knew St. Louis well enough that finding a place to stop for the night wouldn't be too difficult.

On the other hand, there was a little city called Cape Girardeau; a speck on the map with a population of 37,000 and a claim to fame that includes some old houses, a museum, and a state park. Yeah!

We decided to take a chance on the Cape for one reason: a man named Randall. Randall had sent me an email shortly after we announced our road trip, and he was very convincing, offering to organize the whole meet up himself, to mobilize the local press, and to find us lodging. All of this came with the caveat 'I mean, if the whole St. Louis thing doesn't turn out. I don't want to pressure you.'

Friendly *and* not pushy? Randall, you win my friend.

And we made the right choice. From the moment we arrived in Cape Girardeau, we felt incredibly welcome.

Randall invited us over to his house and introduced us to his Filipina wife who he had met and married while traveling around Asia. He told us about his life, what he was working on, and then told us that he had rented us rooms(!) at the newest and fanciest hotel in town. When we got to the hotel, we ooh'd and ahh'd over the luxuriousness of not sleeping on a couch or spare bed in someone's basement, and quickly collapsed, trying to recharge a bit for the Tweetup which was scheduled for a few hours later.

The rest of the night was a bit of a blur, but I remember the highlights: we played tipsy-beach-volleyball in the sand pit behind the bar where the Tweetup was held. My mother (who had driven down with my father from Columbia for the event) won a t-shirt from the Cape's tourism board, and when Andi and I returned to the hotel to crash, Ash ended up staying out, living it up at a basement party in the backwoods of Cape Girardeau.

Randall also made sure that we were well-fed the whole time we were in his town.

When we first arrived, we had a massive lunch prepared by his wife and mother-in-law, consisting of all kinds of noodles and meats, spring rolls, and plantain desserts. It was phenomenal, and not one of us expected to be eating the best Filipino food we had ever tasted in a tiny town in Southeast Missouri.

Before we left, Randall took us out to breakfast and made sure we had heaping helpings of everything before we set off for Columbia.

Our stay ended with group photos with Randall and his wife, and as we left we were grinning like idiots and talking excitedly about what a good time we had had in Cape Frickin' Girardeau.

The Bold Who Built Boulder

When we first pulled into Boulder, Colorado it was crazy-late, and Ash, Andi, and I had to sneak very quietly into local blogger Grace's apartment, which she had generously left open for us, along with the sofa bed pulled out and made up. As had become customary for us when arriving in a new place, we all immediately collapsed, exhaustion outweighing the volume of caffeine we had running through our veins.

The next morning we got our first glimpse of the city. Grace's boyfriend James (who is also a well-known Internet personality) gave us a tour as we walked toward the downtown area through a patch of woods and over a creek that runs through the city. I recorded a short video during this walk, and the first words that came to mind were "Boulder...this is where some people live. Take note New York."

The contrast between Boulder (a place that has become a bit of a Mecca for startups largely because of Techstars, a successful startup incubator/investor that calls Boulder home), and Manhattan (where most new technology-based startups seem to be congregating) was stark. As we wandered around downtown, it became even starker.

James waved to some of the people who buzzed by on their bikes, heading out to the mountainous areas nearby for a little workout during their lunch break. Everywhere I looked, people were tanned, fit, and happy. The air was crisp and clean, and I felt like I had accidentally driven to Northern California due to the city's healthy, nature-focused vibe.

We sat down for a light lunch with a ragtag bunch of local techies, bloggers, entrepreneurs, and social media gurus before heading over to visit the colorfully decorated offices of Lijit, the tech-company Grace worked for.

After chatting with the staff and CEO of Lijit (very friendly people), we checked out one of the offices where companies involved in the Techstars incubator build their empires. We hung out with the guys who started Everlater, a company that helps people build online travel journals.

Afterwards, we went to a nearby coffee shop to talk tech with the founders of Kapost, a pretty brilliant app for organizing and publishing online content.

The vibe at all the companies we visited was one of healthy productivity. Their offices were spartan, and the people we talked to spoke calmly and without the wild-gesticulations of newbie entrepreneurs explaining their ideas. I got a sense the businesspeople of Boulder intended to slowly but surely take over the world, and they were so certain they could, they didn't need to make a big fuss about it.

The day was capped with a party at The Bitter Bar, a local favorite where we were welcomed with a custom menu and access to Mark, the winner of the 2010 Cocktail World Cup (which took place in New Zealand).

Mark and the rest of the über-talented staff whipped up delicious and debilitating concoctions for us all night long, which resulted in our party of 30 or so people shambling out the door when the bar closed, drunkenly making our way to another bar several blocks away.

According to the photos I found on my camera the next day, we had a good time. We laughed, we explored, and we were apparently utterly fascinated by a wrought-iron gate topped with an anatomically correct, smiling-and-waving gargoyle statue.

It's good to have photographic evidence of the important stuff.

Ahab

I shouldn't have panicked, but I did. A little.

Things didn't go as planned, and although that was kind of the point, I didn't expect this.

Two-thirds of the way through our three-person road trip, Ash headed back to Philly and left us without a third member of our trio. We were also without transportation, and in Los Angeles.

She had indicated that this might be a possibility—that there was work back home, that there were money concerns, and that time was becoming an issue—but Andi and I still didn't think she'd actually leave.

We'd already overcome a lot of obstacles, and this one had seemed so small in comparison. Like a spaceship that had deflected asteroids and rival space-lasers, only to be crushed by a falling tree upon return to Earth.

We had places we needed to be. There were things we still had on the agenda, and they were time-sensitive.

That night, we were scheduled to have drinks with a few friends up in San Francisco, and the next day we were going to meet up with Jenny: a fellow blogger, published author, and Google employee. She was going to give us a tour of the Googleplex (Google's famous main campus in Silicon Valley).

Andi, my comrade-in-panic, called up her local contacts while I called mine, but no one was planning on heading up north to the Bay Area for the next several days, so we had no one to hop a ride with.

As a last-ditch effort, we pulled up Craigslist, breezed through the rideshare postings and found a willing party who was heading north. We figured out a fair price, gave him our address and waited to see what we had gotten ourselves into.

A few hours later, a beat-up beige sedan pulled up in front of the house we were staying at, and a curly-haired guy with a smirk the size of most people's full-smile got out and introduced himself.

"I'm going to have to move some stuff around in the backseat," he said. "One minute."

As he moved a dress shirt on a hanger from the window, he reached down below the back seat and pulled out a harpoon gun.

It may sound strange, but the first thing that went through my head was: "Is he robbing us with a harpoon gun?"

The second thing to go through my head was: "It seems like a whole lot of effort to create a post on Craigslist, drive someone out to the middle of nowhere, and then shoot someone with a harpoon gun."

My brain finished with: "It's actually kind of brilliant, but that thing is too cumbersome for him to use in the car, so at least I'd have some warning if he tried anything. Let's see where this goes."

Like a security guard who thinks he glimpsed a reflection from a pistol in somebody's jacket out of the corner of his eye, I spend the duration of the trip with one eye on our driver. We stopped to fill up the tank and I made sure that either Andi or I stuck with the car at all times, and were within shouting distance of other people.

Even if he just drove off with our stuff, we would be in a bad situation. We don't know this guy! And he's got a frickin' harpoon gun! Who knows what he's capable of? He's like some kind of Bond villain, but the one you don't realize is a villain until he's shooting lasers from his ruby-eye or staring at you down the 'barrel' of his harpoon gun. They'd call him 'Ahab' and he would get together with Jaws on weekends and pick up unsuspecting rideshare seekers...

But nothing happened. Other than having to keep up with some bland conversation and listening to myriad of Top 40 stations on the radio, we made it out alive and with all of our bags in tow.

The next day we enjoyed a lovely tour of the Googleplex and were able to bask in the glorious Bay Area weather.

While we were having a meal with a group of Silicon Valley entrepreneurs after the tour, I glanced at a newspaper on the table next to us and my jaw dropped when I saw the headline. It turns out that the night before, two twenty-somethings were picked up by their rideshare driver and left dead on the side of the road. The coroner seems to think the marks on their bodies were made by *a harpoon*!

Just kidding. He was a nice guy.

Drinking in the Moment & a Boot

By the time we reached Portland, Oregon the road trip trio was spent.

Ash had to head back toward the East Coast as soon as we reached Los Angeles, but her shoes were filled by Maren—an entrepreneur/blogger from Reno—when we arrived in San Francisco. But although she joined us late in the game, at this point even Maren was zonked-out from our schedule and all the driving up the West Coast.

A blogger named Brittany welcomed us to Portland and showed us around, explaining that a lot of the skyscrapers and other buildings were very new, and were quite sustainable, as well. Wind turbines jutting out from overhangs and plants lining the roofs supported her assertion.

We indulged in some delicious and creative street food from the cart restaurant scene that is a staple of Portland cuisine, and met up with a dozen or so interesting and enthusiastic folks at a bar well-known for its microbrews.

From there, we trekked over to a legit German pub, where we proceeded to drink a full-sized glass boot full of beer (which is actually a game played with a group of people at this place; I won) and to generally make fools of ourselves in the best way possible.

At this point, however, there was a growing awareness that our grand adventure was almost at an end. I recognized the feeling, as I tend to feel the same way the final month I'm living in a country before moving on to a new home, new language, new group of friends.

It's a sense of impending change, and it's hard to shake. You're a little bit excited to have made it so far, a little bit disappointed that your current lifestyle will be coming to an end, and more than a little anticipatory about what comes next.

We checked out a street festival before saying our goodbyes and watched Portland fade into the distance as we headed off to the final stop on the road trip: Seattle.

It was in Seattle that Maren would leave us, heading back home to Reno, and Andi would return to her normal life (and apartment). I would head to Southeast Asia and spend the next four months living in Thailand.

The worst part about looking forward to the future, I realized, is that sometimes you miss important details in the present.

Seattle was fun, but I knew that I wasn't fully there, I wasn't fully invested anymore, and my mind was already focused on the next step and my next country. Will it be easy to travel around Thailand, using Bangkok as a hub? Will it be easier or more difficult to meet people than in New Zealand? Will I miss a connecting flight on the way, or catch some incurable disease while there? What kind of risks am I taking?

I took stock of my future-facing tendency when I left for Asia so the next time I found myself in Seattle, I would be able to take a few days to simply be in the moment. Even if everything was going to change very soon, I knew it was worth the time to focus on being present and to nurture a sense of now-ness.

If I don't stop and make sure to do this sometimes, I find my thoughts wander off more frequently, and then I miss out on the wonderful Cape Girardeaus and Bitter Bars that life has to offer.

Birthing Businesspeople

Wage Slavery

I've spent a good deal of my life working for cash.

From a very young age I babysat at my family's church or dusted shelves at the local independent bookstore to earn the pocket change I would wad together and thrust at the bespectacled man behind that counter at Walmart. Afterward, I would dreamily shamble home, clutching some newfangled video game in my joystick-nimble hands, imagining myself slaying dragons, blowing things up, and generally running amok in a consequence-free environment.

My motivations to earn changed as I grew older—in college I worked to pay for classes and to be able to take my girlfriend out for dinners and drinks—but the overriding drive remained the same. In order to survive, I needed money, and as much of it as I could get.

There never seemed to be enough! I would get a new job that made more money, then I would start buying more expensive clothes or meals and I'd be further behind than before. The math of the situation didn't seem to add up, and all I knew was that unless I tried something different, I'd be playing a never-ending game of catch-up with myself, until I died like the protagonist in one of my games.

It wasn't until I started working for myself that I figured out how the whole money thing operates, and why, if I kept working for other people, I would never get where I wanted to be.

A paycheck is a funny thing. It's an object of desire, and most people look forward to having one handed to them (I don't know if they imagine blowing stuff up like I did, but to each their own). A person's happiness often hinges on whether or not they get their paycheck at the right time.

Families unravel if paychecks don't arrive regularly. People go on killing sprees if they don't get paid, and I don't mean in a video game. Riots and revolutions are incited and atrocities are committed when people are no longer able to provide for themselves and their families.

Beware the paycheckless, for they are no longer rational human beings.

Or are they?

Among the many tools used to keep society ticking along at a steady clip, paychecks give people a sense of security that is illusory at best, an outright lie at worst. Though we watch for them with the eager eyes of a desert-dweller at a cold glass of water, a paycheck is more anchor than wings.

The Industrial Revolution

Until the Industrial Revolution, most people worked in agriculture or in family trades.

What this means in practical terms is that there were no paychecks. You either lived off the land and money you earned from selling the fruits (or vegetables) of your labor, or you were a blacksmith, butcher, or seamstress; generally whatever your parents were. No paycheck necessary, just food and shelter. Maybe a few bucks to save for a dowry. Those were high times.

And then the machines took over.

Suddenly, skilled labor wasn't necessary because all the complicated stuff was done by mechanical looms and steam engines. People were hired for their ability to obey simple orders ("Don't play in the cement mixer!") and paid accordingly. Less effort to produce more stuff meant cheaper products, faster.

So, there was a production boom. Imagine a marketplace populated only by what people were able to harvest and create with their bare hands, and simple, human-powered machines.

Now picture that same market a decade later, stocked with plenty of clothing, food, and tools, all created in factories. One machine could do the work of 300 people in a third of the time. I can tell you what the tycoons of the day were thinking: "Who the hell is going to buy all this *stuff*?"

Especially in the United States, this was a problem that arose from industry. It didn't make sense to produce less, because the cost of production went down as larger batches were run. At the same time, it wasn't paying off to produce at full capacity because no one was buying. This was a nation of savers, people who had been brought up with a Protestant work-ethic, a tenet of which was to stay financially stable for God and not buy more than necessary.

For these people at this time, necessary wasn't much. They'd been living with very little for so long, it seemed morally abominable to buy things just because they were available and they had the resources to do so. "What for?" they would say. "What I've got now works well enough for me."

Enter Marketing

It was around this time that some clever people realized they could create value out of nothing.

The trouble with the market, in their minds, was that everything was more or less the same. If you wanted oats, you'd saunter over to the general store, walk up to the barrel of oats, and scoop out as much as you needed.

You wouldn't ask if they were Aunty Jane's Famous Oats or if they had anything from the Smith Brothers on hand. Oats were oats, and they sold like oats.

Marketing says otherwise. According to marketing, Smith Brothers Oats are *more* than just oats, they're Smith Brothers Oats. By giving them a name and attaching an implied value to them (with a slogan or just by naming them, while the competitors remain unnamed), these oats can command a higher price. They're premium! Who wants regular oats when you can have Smith Brothers'? Give me two bags.

This trend of branding spread across all industries, and as a result, today you'd be hard-pressed to find a product that hasn't been branded in some way.

So what does marketing and branding have to do with your paycheck? Plenty.

Marketing allows salespeople to do more than just diversify and add implied value to their stock, it allows them to promote products to new audiences, as well. Even within existing audiences, new sales can be made because of the skilled use of what's called a 'unique value proposition,' essentially saying that one product has an advantage over another, similar product.

After marketing emerged, people who had previously felt they were fine with whatever old linens happened to be in the cupboard suddenly weren't so convinced. "These new linens have a higher thread count and a new color that just came out this season. Don't want to get left behind. Better buy a set."

Factory owners found a way to get enough customers to buy everything they could produce, and this led to more factories, which led to more marketing, which led to more sales. Cupboards were bursting with excess linens.

At the same time, folks who were working in factories were earning less and less as the prices of what they were producing dropped due to improvements in technology and infrastructure. These workers took on longer hours and more than one job in order to survive in a world where the cost of living was skyrocketing (because of the increase in marketing) even while the cost of production was dropping.

For the most part, this cycle continues today, and it's an incredibly difficult one to escape. We are tied to our paychecks because they allow us to buy the newest whatever (which is built to become obsolete) and to then replace it with a new whatever next season.

Cars are made to need repairs and replacements (have to keep the automotive industry profitable, after all). Computers are produced with the expectation that they'll be more or less useless within a few years. Clothing is not made to be repaired, but replaced when a button falls off or thread loosens.

In Aldus Huxley's *Brave New World*, there's a saying every citizen is taught as they grow up: "Ending is better than mending. The more stitches, the less riches."

The idea is that you should get rid of a possession when it breaks it rather than attempting a fix yourself. This allows the economy to keep chugging along because more people will need more stuff. As a result, they'll work harder to be able to afford the stuff, and by working, the stuff they (or their peers) buy is produced faster.

That paycheck you receive twice a month is your ticket to participate in this cyclical system.

People wonder why life sometimes seems so meaningless. "Why I am so depressed? I've got everything! The new TV just arrived yesterday, the new room was just finished on the house, and the kids love the trampoline. I can't figure it out."

When personal meaning, self-worth, and happiness are derived from consumption, it's not at all strange when an identity crisis of sorts emerges. What's worse is that making any sort of headway is almost impossible in this kind of system, because in a month or two you'll be behind again when all your stuff is obsolete.

Some people enjoy this process because it's mindless and relatively simple to keep your head above water if you play by the rules. The status quo is just difficult enough to attain that people feel some strain from the effort, but not so difficult that they break a sweat. I refer to this mode of operation as 'flat-lining' because it's steady and right down the middle on a chart that has happiness way up on top and depression down at the bottom. It's contentment, and this is the default reality for most people born in the wealthy world.

Breaking free from it isn't easy and requires a good deal of priority adjustment and legwork. You *will* sweat and you *will* sink down below flat-lining level from time to time. But like any healthy heartbeat, the lows serve to punctuate the highs, and without them you can't muster the momentum to keep leaping and enjoying those epic, intense feelings of happiness most people will never experience.

Wage slavery is economic *and* mental. We're tied to the paycheck that allows us to flat-line and pay for the escapism that helps us ignore the unease we feel at being so depressingly average.

Breaking those bonds can take a while, but it's doable so long as you take the time to notice the chains and look for the weak links.

Asymmetrical Warfare

I'm not a very competitive person.

Or rather, I'm very competitive, but only with myself. I'm constantly striving to beat my last best, and I like to show myself who's boss by getting my initials just a little higher than my last on that Tetris arcade machine, and the numbers a little higher than last month in my bank account.

When I was in school, however, I fell into a very competitive situation that I couldn't seem to get out of.

I went to Missouri State University and dual-majored in Graphic Design and Illustration, and the program was difficult, and hard to get into. You had to be accepted, and there were few slots available (even fewer for dual-majors like myself).

This, of course, led to an atmosphere where everyone knew everyone else, and over the course of a few years we all knew every other student's work, as well. Strengths, weaknesses, color palette preferences—it was all on the table after many critiques.

With few exceptions we were all friends, and I think that only increased the intensity of our undeclared aesthetic rivalries.

There were a lot of very talented people in the program, but there were five who tended to get the highest grades on projects: a group of four guys who often worked and hung out together, and me.

The four other guys were very talented, and each had a decidedly different style than I did. They did beautiful work, and despite all the talented people in the program, I considered them my main competition when it came to getting the high grade on any given project, and for doing the best work (grades aside).

Things escalated when these guys got organized and started producing clever handmade 'zines to spread around town. They moved into a big apartment together, as well, and made it into a studio environment of sorts, increasing their productivity even further. They were kicking ass and making names for themselves, and their work was just getting better as a result.

I felt like I was plateauing in comparison, holding still while they kept moving forward, and I knew I had to figure out how to speed up my pace, and fast.

There were four of them and only one of me, and despite the fact that I can produce an obscene amount of work in a short amount of time when I want to, I knew trying to beat them at their own game would be foolish. Not only did they have an advantage in numbers, but they also had different styles to work with, and were comfortable living as a community, while I'm a firm individualist. No dice.

One thing I did have that they didn't was a job in my field. As far as I could tell, they had only dabbled (as we all had) in freelance work up to that point, while I was actually a legitimate working professional, being paid to design and learn about design. I could use this to my advantage.

When another design job opened up on campus, I submitted my portfolio. I got the job, and started learning more about layout work, production, and dealing with clients; expanding my horizons much further than before.

I then took a job at the design school itself, running the computer and print labs, working as a software specialist for anyone who needed help. More skills gained.

Finally, I started working as a columnist for the University newspaper and as the designer for a new glossy magazine that had just started in my city.

Each of these positions gave me new skills, new resources, new connections, and a much stronger sense of responsibility (not to mention more cash). Using what I had at my disposal, I was able to start my first company (a culture magazine) and then my second (a design and development studio) while still in school.

I had carved out my own niche: businessperson.

While everyone else in my department was still struggling to be the best designer, competing with each other, I pulled away from the contest, happily blazing a new trail, no longer feeling the need to compare my work to theirs. I realized that we all had different purposes, different standards, different reasons for doing what we were doing. Everyone could succeed and be happy according to completely different metrics. This wasn't an option I had ever considered before.

In my mind, there no longer seemed to be a wall between business and design, but instead there was a semi-permeable membrane between these worlds. Both involved creation and innovation, both required big-picture thinking.

My life changed when I discovered this professional hybridization, and I started to consider myself my main competition once more. All it took was a reanalysis of priorities and figuring out which game I actually wanted to be playing in the first place.

A Relationship of Words

OkCupid

From: Shannonmenon
Message: I bet your inbox is almost as full as mine...

Hey, I'm Shannon. I also share your joy of kicking life's ass and going to cultural events, which unfortunately means I often go alone because most people are lame.

So I swore off contacting guys on the 'cupe because they never write me back (can you believe that? I blame the hunter instinct, but you seem to be different, so I thought what the hell, I need an art party partner in crime).

I'm an abstract painter and entrepreneur (such a generic term, I have an amazing idea to change the face of urban areas as we know it...seriously), and hopefully next summer I will be a resident of France for a couple months to travel around Europe and do live painting.

Anyway, check out my profile; on top of being awesome and talented, I'm also unconventionally conventionally hot, and we all know hot people don't have to stand in line at events.

* * *

Holla 'atcha girl,
  -Shannon

PS: I'm starting a badminton league, so come handle some cock with me...shuttlecock that is.

Gchat

5:49 AM

Shannon: whoa hi, wish i had time to chit chat, freelancing like a mofo doing crappy graphic design... but Hi anyways

Me: well hey! fancy meeting you here

Shannon: right? what brings you round the gchat parts at this early hour?

Me: checking email...just got back from watching a movie, the one with that gal from Juno in it, and just about to start putting together a project for tomorrow

Shannon: LOL

Shannon: I once peed in front of that chick from juno, true story

Me: intentionally? as a statement? was she the catalyst for said peeing?

Shannon: hahaha no, 3 cups of joe were the culprits, but i did get the satisfaction of walking up to her, seeing her prepare to say "sure ill give you a signature" but instead i walked up... straight faced...and said..."they have run out of TP you may wanna go ask for more."

Email

From: Colin
　　To: Shannon
　　Message: Wanna go to this thing?

Hey Shantastic!

So I got this invite the other day and I realized

1. I'd be in town for it
　　2. So would you (I think)
　　3. You're an artist, so you likely don't mind galleries
　　4. I love galleries
　　5. These are always filled with interesting people
　　6. I could ask you out to it, and maybe for a get-together ahead of time (so our first in-person meeting isn't at a pseudo-networking event). Do you have work or some such tomorrow? If so, what time are you off?
　　7. Oh yeah, and do you have a car? This place is in Venice, so I guess it all depends if you want to head over to the Westside.
　　8. I should warn you now that I think lists are hilarious. So yeah. This.
　　9. Free booze.
　　10. Let me know!

From: Shannon
　　To: Colin
　　Message: RE: Wanna go to this thing?

* * *

1. yes you will :)
    2. yes i am!
    3. no i don't mind them, in fact i quite like them =)
    4. must be part of our OKC match %
    5. <3 interesting people
    6. I am working, on the west side in el segundo! we can meet up on my lunch break... yogurt land perhaps? im off at 630ish i can bail a bit early if need be.
    7. have car can travel... david bowie cd in the player, lets rock
    8. Speak list to me baby oh yeah!
    9. Yes please
    10. its on

Email to a Friend

...I went out with a gal I met online a few months ago the other day, and we had a pretty good time, despite everything that could go wrong going wrong.

We snagged lunch earlier in the day, and the conversation was great, but we had to cut it a little short, as she had to get back to work down in El Segundo, and construction on the roads was...well, pretty much how it always is on the West Side. Horrendous. Terrible. Torturous. Food was good, though, and the company was top-notch. Seemed like a cool chick.

Later that night we went to a gallery event that ended an hour before we arrived. We walked around Venice a bit before realizing that everything was closed. A few drinks were had. Public urination was involved. She ended up curled up with me on the couch I was crashing on in my friend's living room. When he got up in the morning for work, he played the whole thing off very well. Good friends like that are hard to come by.

The next date was interesting, as we had some drinks, engaged in amazing conversation and fooled around a bit, but I had decided to go running on the beach earlier in the day which resulted in an impressive and painful full-body sunburn. The result was a kind of masochistic pleasure and pain situation; the kind of thing that some people pay good money for, but that I would have preferred to be less of the latter.

I'm leaving for Thailand soon, and she's the kind of girl who I think I'll stay good friends with. I love making those kinds of connections...

A Later Email

From: Shannon
   To: Colin
   Message: f ya

T.hubbs hunny babe lemme preface by saying I'm drunk. It was the 100k facebook fan party at my work oh wait 105k facebook fans yeah I have an army. Anyways the news I had to tell u we just hired a director of marketing who used to work for that big date site... knows one of the guys in charge of okcupe I gave him a light over veiw of 'around the world in 80 dates' and said the dude would be totes be into it... add in a grain of salt... he woould he interested... we need to persue this. Ok I'm off too get laid slash sleep baiiii xo

From: Colin
   To: Shannon

Dude, I LOVE drunk emails from you!

Haha, let me know if any movement is made on the around the world gig, and I'm in.

Hope you had good sex + sleep! Talk soon!

Chapter 6: A Falang Walks in the Park

12.10.2010 — 1st Page of My Notebook, Bangkok, Thailand

I never write on the first page of a notebook, but I'll never be able to say that again.

Sure, I'll write little word bubbles or a clever bit of poetry that comes to mind, but certainly not anything important.

And now, of course, the pressure is on to write something really meaningful and memorable. Let's start with this:

You have only one life in which to fulfill your every ambition. Act accordingly.

Fish Balls

I was standing awkwardly with a sack of fish balls in my hand when I first saw her.

The setting was as such:

The humidity was oppressive, which I had come to learn meant one of the torrential downpours that bombard Bangkok daily during monsoon season was imminent.

People were walking by, sluggishly moping through their day, seemingly without a care in the world. I discovered early on the locals walk as if moving through molasses even if their house is on fire.

Most of the food vendors were starting to pack up their wares, recognizing they would be drenched in about 15 minutes if they didn't, and not wanting to go home with no money *and* no food. Tiny tacos made from cornmeal and whipped cream were wrapped in foil, bits of unidentifiable meat on sticks were locked away into metal heating cabinets built into the carts. Spring rolls were dropped into plastic Tupperware containers to be fried and sold after the storm had passed.

And while I stood there, looking and feeling quite grungy (I refer to it as my 'Hemingway' look, because it makes me feel classier about not shaving/bathing/changing clothes very often), the most gorgeous girl I had ever seen walked over and stood beside me, obviously waiting for me to finish my transaction. The first thing that jumped into my mind was "Oh crap, Colin, you've somehow managed to mess up the money-for-food transaction and offended a Thai supermodel."

Thankfully, that wasn't the case.

Before I was able to finish paying for my freshly bagged, fried fish balls (I should clarify they were balled up fish—like spherical fish sticks—not the testicles of a barracuda), she said "You are Colin? You are the traveler!"

I'm pretty sure my jaw dropped, as this was the last thing I expected her to say, much less in English.

The part of town I lived in and the part of town where this story takes place is near Victory Monument. Though tourists do gather over by the Monument itself, the side streets are very Thai-centric, and you don't encounter a lot of English-speakers or white-people (*falang*). Most days I wouldn't see anyone except locals, which is why I chose to live where I did.

I realized I let an uncomfortable amount of time pass while recovering from my shock, and managed to stutter "Uh...yeah...?" I didn't really know what was going on.

"I have read your blog and know you are here, and you are!" She said it the same way I would picture a young wizard excitedly telling his friends about a new spell he had learned. "I said the incantations, dropped in some eye of newt, and boom! Summoned a gargoyle. He's sleeping in my sink!"

"Yeah, I am. Ah, hello!" I reached out for a handshake and she awkwardly placed her hand in mine, clearly aware of what she was supposed to do but not at all practiced in the mechanics of it. The handshake is not terribly popular in Thailand.

She explained how her friend—who was going to school in California—reads my blog and told her I was in Bangkok and living in the Victory Monument district. She had been watching for me in the off chance we'd cross paths; and we did, wonder of wonders.

"What a small world!" I said as she put her arm through mine after bullheadedly insisting on paying for my fish balls and handing the man manning the cart two 10-baht coins.

What the hell is going on? I thought. This feels like the intro of a very niche porno, where the hot girl comes on to the ragged guy while he's visiting another country and buys him fish balls. Does this kind of thing really happen? What *is* happening?

After answering a few of the standard questions ("Do you *really* travel to a new country every few months?" "Do you *really* only own 50 things?"), she told me a bit about herself, and I liked her more and more.

She worked in marketing, but was still in school for it. She enjoyed the challenge of communicating messages to people she'd never met.

To pay for school she did some modeling, mostly catalogs but also some runway work when the opportunity arose. She told me a bit about the local fashion industry when I asked, and about some of the trials and tribulations she'd been through getting her first few gigs.

"What really got me started, though, was that the surgeon I have been going to for my operation is the same doctor who does work on a lot of the big, famous models, and he told some agents about me."

"What operation is that?"

"Oh, because I am becoming woman. I was born a boy."

For the second time in less than 10 minutes, I was dumbstruck.

I knew all about the "ladyboy" situation in Thailand. It's a big deal, and people visit from all over the world to engage in some, ah, ladyboy activities.

I had also been told they could be convincing, but up until this point, although I had seen some very beautiful women who were not women, I could tell the difference. There was some indication in how they walked or how they were built or *something* that indicated perhaps some physical editing had occurred.

This girl I was talking to, however, showed nothing to indicate she wasn't what she appeared to be. Everything was damn-near perfect, and the first thought that rolled through my head when I grasped what she was saying was "Impressive work!"

She told me a little about her transformation, and how her main surgery would begin soon, but that she had already had the top done, and some minor adjustments to her face.

We had sat down in a park partway through the conversation, but after dropping that bombshell she told me she had to get to work and that it was great talking to me. I thanked her for the fish as she left, but she was clearly in a hurry, whether because she had divulged more than she had planned or because she wanted to avoid the worst of the rain, I don't know.

The rest of the day I walked around in a bit of a daze. Questions kept rolling through my mind, things I had never really thought about before.

Could I be into a girl who was post-op? Someone who was physically a girl, even if she hadn't been born that way?

What if I didn't know and found out only after we had fooled around? What if I found out *in bed*? How would I respond to that? If I really liked her, would I see her again?

Strangely, I found myself having very few answers, and could only come to the conclusion it would depend on the situation. This person who had whisked into my life, bought me some fish balls and upped my confidence a bit by being attractive and flirty and interesting and interested was, in her mind—and at this point in *most* of her body—female.

Who am I to say she wasn't just a girl who was born with the wrong genitalia? Isn't what's going on in her mind the most important part?

It's a tricky question, and I doubt I would have even thought twice about it had I not been interested in her to begin with.

I realized I had stopped in the middle of the sidewalk mid-thought, and as I finished my sack of fish balls, I slowly walked back toward my apartment, a little confused and ever-so-slightly satisfied with the day.

Not Today

I am not going to shave today. No fucking way.

I'll shower. I'll brush my teeth. I'll be a human being. That's as much as I can promise. As much as I *will* promise.

No interviews today. Not unless you want to hear a grizzly man's entrepreneurial advice.

No meetings. No work. I think I'll walk to the store and buy a bag of Doritos and eat the whole thing.

I might play a video game. I can *get* a video game. These are things I can do. I have the right. You can't stop me.

If I don't touch my hair today, no one will recognize me. With this week's growth of beard and some baggy clothing I could take off down the street and all anyone would remember is that it was cold today, and something happened but they don't remember what. I am of the shadows. I am invisible to the human eye.

I'll adjust my body language and posture so my hands remain in my pockets and my elbows are pulled tight against my body. My eyes will remain downcast, watching the pavement in front of me as I meander to and fro', not a care in the world, no one knowing my name.

Sunglasses would be a giveaway, so I'll just squint against the early afternoon sun as I hobble about town, belly full of snack food and mind wandering aimlessly, no focal point needed or wanted.

I won't smile. I won't speak clearly. I'll mumble thank you's and hello's when necessary, but won't engage in conversations any longer than a few syllables.

No parties tonight. No hobnobbing with political royalty or economic dukes and duchesses. I'll be at home watching a movie I've already seen on my laptop in my room with the door locked and my headphones turned way up.

I'll experience a condensed range of emotions. I'll mentally engage not at all. I'll be recognized not once and contribute not one bit to the world as a whole. I'll run from everything and everyone, but I won't need to pick up my pace to do it. I'll hide in plain sight like I did without even trying so many years ago.

Until tomorrow. I'll see you then.

Blog Life

Ode to Me-Too

When I started blogging as more than just a hobby, the scene was quite different than it is now.

That's not to say there have been truly radical changes these past few years, but within the small percentage of people on the planet who blog to make money or otherwise build an asset, there has been a fairly large shift in technique and strategy.

What people are writing about has also changed a good deal since back then, and there are a lot of 'me-too' bloggers today, whereas just a few years ago many topics were handled by just a small handful of passionate writers, each with their own unique voice.

Today, though, most of what's available seems to be a copy of a Xerox of something that's already been done, which is a little sad, but probably also necessary. Do I need to read one more post about why Tyler Durden is a (insert theme of blog here)? Not particularly. Will another pithy Top 32 list help me one bit? Unlikely.

But all the hubbub and activity is necessary to form the intellectual stew that will eventually give birth to new species, and what you tend to see is a thousand me-too's hopping on board with a trusted topic, and then six months later all but a few have died off. Those few survivors who managed to hang on have at that point started to come into their own, expanding out in different directions than they were originally going and usually coming up with some really solid work.

I feel like I can say this with some authority because I myself was one of those me-too bloggers for many months, and it took a while before I got a solid grasp on what it was I could write about that other people would find interesting, valuable, and hard to copy.

Origin

It's fun to look back and think about how small my blogging posse was when I first started out.

I decided if I was going to become known and get a decent number of subscribers, I would need to connect with other people who were talking to the kind of audiences I wanted to attract. I soon found these people were good for more than just associative branding—they happened to also be interesting, and to be doing interesting things—so in many cases we became fast friends.

There were few people who had been writing about topics like personal-development, lifestyle design, location independence, and that kind of thing for any amount of time, but the few that had were generally very open and encouraging.

I sent out an email to Chris Guillebeau (now one of the more successful pro-bloggers out there) pretty early on, and his positive and friendly response motivated me to shoot out emails to a few other bloggers whose work I had enjoyed and learned from.

I started talking to Corbett Barr (who runs the very successful Think Traffic blog) just a few months in, after he sent me an email thanking me for a comment I left on his site.

A big part of my strategy at this point was leaving well-written comments on other blogs I liked, thinking (1) it would get the attention of the author (like it did with Corbett), and (2) it would encourage people to check out my blog if they liked what I had to say.

This strategy worked pretty well at the time, though these days it doesn't seem to have the same impact (I stopped paying much attention to comments, except those left on my blog, a long time ago, and I know many other people who have done the same. The conversation just doesn't evolve the way it should using that format anymore, and I'm convinced something better will come along soon).

It was around this time I first made contact with Cody McKibben, a blogger who I would meet in person a year-and-a-half later in Thailand, but to whom I was often compared in the early days of Exile Lifestyle.

Cody had been writing about living and working from where you want for a long time and he was good about outlining productivity tips as well, which was something I tended to write about a lot. Getting good responses from this small group led to a whirlwind of online networking.

I connected and started up dialogues with bloggers from all over the world. Amber Zuckswert, Sean Ogle, David Walsh, Robert Granholm, Dirk de Bruin, Jon Bardos, Adam Baker, Josh Hanagarne, Ash Ambirge, Maren Kate Donovan, and many others. We had all started blogging with conviction within a few months of each other, and we kind of grew in parallel though along different paths, like different kinds of plants in the same garden.

We helped each other grow with suggestions and connections and by sending traffic each other's way. There was also an understanding we all shared, which helped on a different level. Each and every one of these people was looking for something—was trying to break away from one lifestyle to build a new one—and when everyone else in your life treats your ambition like some kind of pipe-dream, it's satisfying to have a conversation with another person (even if they live hundreds of miles away) who just *gets* it, no convincing or apologizing necessary.

Over time, we each started reaching what seemed to be a fairly standard tipping point within the blogging field: the 500 subscriber mark.

At that point, you go from being someone who has *some* readers to someone who has a significant number of readers which tend to form a self-sustaining community. The growth begins to picks up organically, you start getting a lot more social media love and people talking about your work. You also have a much more refined sense of who you are and what you're writing about.

I knew from the beginning I would need to set myself apart in order to succeed and make the kinds of connections I wanted to make internationally, so I started branding myself along with my blog, and paid to have some wicked photos taken by my friend Cris, a photographer, entrepreneur, and roller derby girl I had met in Los Angeles. These photos helped me tell my story and make my goals clear (photos of me working on a laptop in Chinatown, on a mountain, on the beach, etc), but also gave the site an air of professionalism that would have taken much longer to achieve otherwise.

Because of the strange, experimental nature of my story, I was also able to garner attention from media and other blogs fairly early on, which is tough to do unless you've really refined your message, generally over a great deal of time.

The concept of moving to a new country every four months based on the votes of perfect strangers is such a great vicarious-living tale that within a month of launching my blog, I was doing interviews for travel podcasts, business blogs, and personal development books. This brought in more traffic and gave me more exposure and incoming links, which helped shoot me up the search rankings faster than I probably deserved.

Well That Was Easy

I look back at some of my early milestones now, and it all seems so simple.

Of course building awareness within other communities will help bolster the ranks of your own. Of course collaborating with guest posts and writing free ebooks will bring in more traffic and help refine your brand. Of course it's better to write about something no one else is writing about, or about something familiar in a different way.

But although Problogger (a massive and successful blog about blogging) was operational several years ago, it wasn't nearly so popular as it is now, so the little things that are taken for granted by even the greenest digital scribbler today were still new ground to tread and anything but proven back then.

There were heated debates about the value of guest posting, for example, and whether using Google Adsense or some other ad-based program was best for generating revenue (I should note there weren't many people arguing against ads on your site at this point in time).

Although back in the day people realized there was money to be made in blogging, most people didn't know how. The existing models of the day were all about banners and text ads, and so that's what the rest of us experimented with (though I am proud to say I decided from day one never to put an advertisement on Exile Lifestyle).

It was a Wild West of sorts, and though it seems strange to think about it now, most businesspeople were just starting to hear the word 'blog' and wondering what that could possibly mean.

We weren't the first generation of bloggers, but we were the first generation to have seen the possibilities in becoming a professional blogger, and to have a vast number of cheap and free resources available that made building a blog easy, even for a non-developer.

We all thought we would get hundreds of thousands of eyeballs on our work, and then somehow leverage those eyes or sell that attention to the highest bidder.

Little did we know the space would become so saturated that one had to work *really* hard to keep attention once you got it. Additionally, it was becoming clearer and clearer that the few revenue models we knew about wouldn't work for everyone.

I ultimately decided—after several months of intending to make Exile Lifestyle itself into a business—to instead use it as a platform for other businesses; a way to draw in new prospects, try out new ideas, and generally raise awareness for anything I chose to do in the future.

This model worked a whole lot better for me, as I hate advertising and hate sales pitches. I'm at my best when I don't have to sell anything to anyone and can just live my life the best way I know how and draw others in by telling them what I'm up to and what I learned from it.

Fortunately, this turned out to be a good choice, as it has allowed me to continue earning money outside the blog instead of investing all of my effort in turning the site itself into a money-maker.

Unfortunately, many other really great blogs have fallen prey to this tradeoff and eventually lost their legitimacy with readers by becoming little more than a sales page. The relationships they were building became very one-way, and when the ratio of 'here, have this' to 'here, buy this' loses its equilibrium, readers find little reason to stick around.

Bloggers create content and trade it for their readers' attention. As with any relationship, blogger/reader interactions remain healthy only when the exchange of value is equal.

* * *

Don't Call Me Blogger

Occasionally I'm hired to do some one-off travel writing gigs, and sometimes I'm brought on to produce pieces on a more consistent basis, too. The title travel writer seems so limiting to me though, since I tend to focus as much on the people and socioeconomics of a place as the travel destinations. But somehow the title sticks and I keep getting hired by travel publications to reminisce about my time on the road.

I don't like being called a 'blogger' any more than I like being called a 'travel writer.' I don't make money directly from my blog, though I guess I do spend a good deal of time working on it. I really prefer to think of myself as an entrepreneur who blogs, though that doesn't fit as nicely on a business card.

I guess being called a blogger wouldn't be the worst thing ever. The blog world is an interesting one, even if an unlikely one. To me, the most interesting thing about blogging, if you look back to the early 2000's when it began to go mainstream, is that it became popular at all.

Blogs started out as digital journals which then evolved into *public* digital journals. That little shift led to a situation where the press was no longer the only voice heard in important discussions, and where any person could become as influential as a politician, religious leader, or celebrity just by making their thoughts available for consumption.

I often wonder what the next step is going to be, after blogging numbers start to sag even more than they already have. I don't think the blog or bloggers will go away any time soon, assuming they ever go away, but I think there will be a next step, just as diaries led to open diaries led to blogs. What will blogs lead to?

Whatever it is I want to be ready for it, and not held back by the too-specific titles I'm given.

Sex Trade

If I were to say "I understand the sex trade in Thailand," I'd be simplifying things to a criminal degree.

It would be much closer to the truth to say "I understand why people participate in the sex trade in Thailand, and can appreciate the benefits and value exchange taking place from both sides of the equation." To expound upon my position while maintaining a family-friendly rating, I could also add "Though, I would never participate in such a trade myself."

There are many countries in the world where prostitution is legal. New Zealand is one of them, and as I understand it, the industry is heavily regulated and all people involved in the transaction walk away with what they want in the end, including the government, which taxes the sex worker's fees.

In Thailand it's a bit different since prostitution is technically illegal; though you wouldn't know it wandering through some parts of Bangkok. From what I'm told, there are a decent number of Thai officials with a financial interest in keeping the sale of sex available and popular (that is, they've got political pimps in office), and because of this, although officially trading nookie for *baht* is illegal, it's tolerated and regulated to a certain degree.

But I don't want to discuss the sex trade, because frankly the whole sad situation just frustrates and depresses me. In countries all over the world people are being kidnapped by deviants or sold into sexual slavery by their family, and despite a good deal of effort exerted toward awareness-building activities and solutions, the practice continues unabated.

What I do want to discuss is how the concept of sex for money has become entwined with regular Thai society, despite the fact that most people in the country have nothing to do with it.

The unfortunate reality for Thai citizens is that unless they are a high-flying executive of some sort, they usually make very little money. The gap between have's and have-not's is astounding, and it's evident everywhere you look. This discrepancy has led to a situation in which people know how life *should* be (they can see it right there, in color, on their TV screens), but don't have the means to reach the heights they aspire to. A low-income shop operated by a family will bring in just enough for them to eat, maybe to buy an old second-hand television set, which will in turn allow them to wallow even more in the discordant reality of their situation.

There is one opportunity available to some locals, however, and it allows them to take a giant economic leap forward.

Walking through certain parts of Bangkok, or lounging about at a decently priced bar around the city, you'll come across more than a few aesthetically unbalanced couples, in this case almost always meaning an older, usually overweight white guy with a young, petite Thai girl. The sight might catch you off-guard the first time you see it, but after a while it becomes so common you don't even look twice.

The mechanics of this kind of relationship are fascinating. Generally what happens is some variation of the following:

The guy visits Thailand, usually on business but sometimes on vacation, and ends up at what's known as a *falang* bar, which means it's marketed toward foreigners who are visiting the city or expats who have moved to the area. There the guy meets a cute girl who seems interested in him, buys her a few drinks and feels like they really hit it off. Numbers are exchanged and plans are made for a date.

On the date, the couple heads out to a nice place—an impressive restaurant in an upscale mall, for example—and the man pays for everything, including a cute dress the girl fawns over on the way to the restaurant. All in all, it's a pretty good night and another date is arranged.

Eventually things get physical, though it may take a few more dates before anything serious happens.

At some point, the guy has to leave—either his business in the area is finished or his vacation is over—and the girl makes it clear she wants him to stay, but that she understands and will wait for him. They start to have frequent Skype conversations, and a long-distance relationship of sorts is formed.

Now, in many cases, this is where things get really interesting and complicated. As the couple are going back and forth with each other on Skype, the girl mentions her mother has gotten sick, or her scooter has broken down and it's hard for her to get to work; at which point the guy is able to swoop in and help out, wiring money to her account and being her knight in shining armor.

What he doesn't know is that her mother wasn't sick and her scooter didn't break down. He also doesn't know she called him just 20 minutes after she was on Skype with another guy she was seeing a few months before he met her, and she was telling this other guy a similar story.

I remember hearing about this method of *Falang-milking* (which is what I've come to call it: I don't know if they have an official term for this routine) from a few friends and I assumed it was an exaggeration. But I started to hang out in the restaurant on the ground floor of my apartment building when the internet would crash in my room, and found there was plenty of evidence that it was indeed commonplace.

What I saw was a handful of girls, none of whom knew each other (as far as I could tell), each coming into the restaurant (which was empty except for me most of the time, since it was the tourism low season) and running through a script with a series of guys on the other end of Skype calls. Each girl had a laptop (which was purchased for them by one of their Skype-buddies) and each used almost the exact same phrases and rhythms, so much so that at the end of the week *I* could easily snag myself a middle-aged Western guy by working through the same, now-memorized routine; if I could only get the accent and cute mispronunciations down.

"Helllllloooo sexxxyy. I looove yoouu. How have you beeeen? I have not been talking to other boys because I know you not like me talking to other boys, but I am so lonely and I am wanting a kitten to keep me company while you are gone. I am looking for a kitten but they are too expensive so I can't get a kitten and I'm lonely. I miss you so much sexxxxyyy. Maybe I get two kitteeeennnsss."

I asked around but wasn't able to find out if there actually was some kind of cheat-sheet these girls were using containing the most effective phrases to say and stories to tell. And unfortunately, I couldn't ask the girls themselves, as a white guy asking them about it would have brought on a string of denials rather than the inside scoop.

After a while it was almost too much for me to listen to. These young women were so blatantly lying, so obviously hustling these guys that hearing them tell these fabrications over and over again, with the clear intention of getting more money from these saps, made me want to run back upstairs, broken WiFi or not.

There were just a few other people living in my building, and four or five of them were middle-aged, overweight white guys, each with cute little Thai girlfriends less than half their age. When I started hanging out downstairs, I would sometimes get locked into conversations with them, and seeing them interact with the girls they were dating made something abundantly clear: they knew what was going on and they were okay with it. Some were so okay with it, in fact, that they allowed themselves to become fully invested in the relationship, just like a normal one.

One of my fellow white-guy apartment building residents told me his story. He was dating a woman back home in the US who had broken his heart, and so he took a vacation to Thailand to get her off his mind. At 45-years-old he met a girl (and I mean that in the most literal sense; I think she was maybe 20, and they had been dating for a few years) whom he fell for. He ended up going back home and selling most of his stuff while having the rest shipped to Bangkok. Now, he explained to me, they're oh so happy together. He takes her out and buys her things, while she sleeps with him and makes him feel great about himself. He's never felt younger and more attractive, he told me.

Another guy who lived down the hall from me told me his story. His girlfriend was a 'good girl,' he said (the term the girls use for themselves when reassuring their *falang* boyfriends they aren't sleeping around). Further, he told me, she loved his big belly ("It reminds her of the Buddha, the girls here love it!") and liked that he was older ("They're not into younger guys, they like older guys here!"). Then he added, with a sly grin, "Of course, by the third date I had her legs behind her head."

At first these stories were just as repugnant to me as the scenario from the girl's side: men who are deluding themselves into thinking these girls like them for more than just their money. Failing at relationships in the US, they move to a place where they aren't required to have a real relationship with a partner, but instead opting for what amounts to having a familiar sex worker on retainer; ready and willing to be on their arm or on their, ah, other arm, and all it takes is money.

I was outraged, but then I realized what a hypocrite that made me.

How many relationships back in the States work this same way, I thought? I may think it makes you morally bankrupt to exchange money for sex and attention, but I could name a dozen people in couplings that work essentially the same way in lots of different countries. Hell, the institution of marriage was largely created to instigate this type of partnership, as back in the day it made good sense to divide up the responsibilities of child-bearing and money-earning. Marriage for love (in its modern meaning) didn't come about until much, much later.

Further, isn't every relationship based on the exchange of value? I know I'm looking for a particular exchange while dating (even if not money for sex), so who am I to criticize what others may be looking for? It would be different, of course, if one person was being coerced into doing something they didn't want to do, but in this case the guys get to feel like sex gods and the girls get to move up in society and help feed their families. That's not a terrible trade, when you think about it.

Of course if we want to get a little meta, it could be argued there *is* coercion involved, because these young women have very few real options if they want to be upwardly mobile. Because of this sad economic reality, finding themselves a foreign guy with money is the easiest road to success.

But in a way that's like saying 'we shouldn't allow people to fish here, because eventually we'll have plenty of farms built to feed everybody, and we don't want to set a bad precedent.' It's a nice idea for the future, but the realities and needs of today outweigh future ambitions in both cases. People need food in order to live, and the promise of food tomorrow won't keep them from starving to death in the meantime. In this case, these girls need money today, regardless of the source, though hopefully in the future they'll be able to earn money in a less potentially coercive way.

I like to think I have a fairly liberal view on relationships and dating, but when situations like this come up I find I'm still stuck in a very small box. The inherent power imbalance of the situation makes me uncomfortable, and I just can't get over how *wrong* it all feels.

Which is good, I think, because it shows I do have some lines drawn in the sand I don't think should be crossed; but it's also something I think I need to work on, because I want to make sure those lines are flexible enough to allow me to learn about all options available before they snap and disappear or forcefully pull me back to my ethical comfort zone before I'm able to learn anything.

Perhaps I just need to talk to more people and find out what they think about relationships, so as to round out my view.

I'd better go stock up on kittens so I can afford their time.

12.19.2010 — Notebook, Midflight, Bangkok to Singapore

Of the incredibly large number of things that I have learned over the years,
 I thank my lucky stars for just one of them every day of the week:

That no matter what happens—and to whom—the world will bounce back
 to its original state. And all the heroes who have been borne by the masses
 will be reborn when they die.

And the villains won't die all the way and will be back for another episode,
 but will be defeated time and time again by the pure of heart and you and me,

and our many sponsors and the good people in the studio audience
 who will laugh and cry

and dance and die
on command,
but won't be owned.

Life In-Transit

In 16 hours, you'll be home.

This is what you repeat over and over again as you pack everything up and start planning how you'll get to the airport. Should you take the monorail? Would a taxi be better? How early should you leave to allow for traffic or a monorail driver strike? Later, as you stand just inside the lobby doors, carry-on bag on the floor next to your feet, you mentally rifle through your options.

It's not a long trip, not really. You've been on rickety, old buses driving through deserts for almost five times as long in the past; and at least on a plane you'll have food and a few functioning bathrooms. Also, they've got standards: laws and regulations which will make the trip moderately uncomfortable at worst, and you can do moderately uncomfortable. When you live life in-transit, moderately uncomfortable can be luxurious.

The hard part won't be the stiff joints or cramped legroom, though. You've done this enough times to know the difficult part is what's going on in your head. The opposing fronts of 'I can't wait to get home' and 'I can't believing I'm leaving all of this behind' swirling and forming a mental tornado, ripping the roof off your thought-processes for the duration of the trip and for about 48 hours after you arrive at your destination.

You tell yourself, 'I'm going to spend this flight writing. A whole 16 hours to write! No distractions! No responsibilities! A month's worth of blog posts finished. Maybe a draft of a novel or some kind of screenplay, I've never written a screenplay.'

But you don't spend too much time thinking about your options because you know you'll end up sleeping as much as possible, instead. And the sleep won't be satisfying because you'll wake up every 20 minutes from turbulence or because the person sitting in the adjacent seat has their headphones turned up too loud while watching a guy-flick full of explosions and screams. Drinks will be served every so often, as well, and you know it's important to stay hydrated while flying. Don't want to miss out on the free cups of water.

Your waking moments will be filled with reel-to-reel brain playbacks of events and conversations you had during the four month-long lifetime you're leaving behind. What's changed since you arrived? In the world? In your business? In your personality? So much. You're a different person once again, sitting and wondering how many cocoons each individual is allotted before they die.

At least you're better for it.

Right? Yeah. You're better. You learned so much. You can say things in other languages. You start to wrap your mouth around some foreign words to prove it when another thought slams into place: you didn't learn enough. You should have learned more. You had this opportunity to learn, and you could have become an expert—a local!—but instead you were working and partying and going on dates. Why didn't you take the language classes that were offered? Why didn't you spend more time engaging with locals or looking for work in town, so you could have seen that side of things? Why didn't you live in a bigger/smaller/cheaper/more expensive apartment? Why didn't you have a flat-mate? Then you *really* would have learned. God you suck at this.

But no, you counter. You did learn. You took away things from the experience few others would be able to figure out. You quantified qualifiers and pieced together puzzles. The relationships you formed are of the highest quality, and the connections you made will last forever. You did it right. You couldn't have done any better. You rule. At life.

Think of the stories you can tell! Everyone will wonder what you did and where you got that scar and how did you possibly live under such circumstances. Do they hate America? Was the food as good as everyone says? You know, and everyone *knows* you know.

You'll spend the next few months answering questions and being 'that person' who got out. Who fled not *from* something, but *toward* something. Such will be your legacy.

And before you know it you'll be on another flight—this time it will only be for a dozen-or-so hours, which you'll casually brush off as an easy ride, much to the shocked delight of those around you—and this moment will come back to you, when you were leaving your last home to go back to your former home, before heading to your new home. You'll flash back and wink at yourself through time and say *everything will be great, you'll see. Trust me, I'm from the future.* And you *will* trust you, because you decided long ago that if you're ever able to time travel, you most certainly will do so, and you'll go back and tell yourself about impending events, but not anything too important.

Right now, though, you need to drag your bag out that door, into the murky, sweaty air, and make your way to the airport: the Alpha and Omega of every story you have to tell.

Chapter 7: International Holiday

Breaking Shells, Breaking Up

Rachel

It would be hard to accurately describe how I felt the first time I found out a girl had a crush on me.

Startled maybe. Shocked. Dumbstruck.

Flummoxed.

It was 9th grade, and up until the day my friend Heather told me that my other friend Rachel was interested in me *like that*, I was 99% certain I would never, ever, under any circumstances, get laid.

I just couldn't picture a scenario where sex would occur. I knew how it worked for most people, and I just couldn't put myself in their shoes. My life was so different, my personality and hobbies suited for a lifelong-gamer not a ladies' man, or even a regular guy who could attract ladies.

One of those jerks with nice clothes and hair that looked intentional.

Maybe a geeky gamer chick, I thought, and that was what I held out for. The kind of gal who would be perfectly happy hanging around all weekend in front of the TV as we enthusiastically blasted each other to bits during marathon sessions of Goldeneye, pausing only to make out.

There might even be tongue involved; the sky's the limit! Who knows?

And being so certain of this, I carefully made it clear to anyone who would listen that I wasn't interested in pursuing anything with anyone. I wasn't being ignored, I was ignoring. Everyone. I could start dating, I would imply, but I'm far too busy leveling my Fighter-Mage character on Ultima Online, and that shit does not come easy. Takes some serious stat-mining and guild-joining and...damn, I wanted to have sex though.

But then Rachel liked me and my whole perspective shifted.

Could it be that I actually stood a chance? That if I were to play the only game I'd never played, evolutionary biology, maybe I could win? Or at the very least, not lose?

This is something I had never considered. I thought it over one day while lasering some Zerglings into cinders with an army of cloaked Wraiths, and came to a decision: I would roll the dice (not the 20-sided kind, this time) and see what happened.

I crossed my fingers, wishing I had some kind of Elven Cloak (for the +3 Charisma), because I would need it.

A year later, well after Rachel and I had started dating, like so many teenagers involved in their first relationship I was already thinking we'd get married someday. That's how it works. We actually brainstormed baby names one weekend, and all of hers were derived from Chopin songs and Native American tribes; it was adorable.

But Rachel had some major baggage in the form of a drug-dealer ex, which led her to have vivid nightmares about him hunting her down, kidnapping her, beating her up, injecting her with drugs, etc. It happened frequently enough that I started to resent this faceless menace who wouldn't leave my girlfriend's dreams alone so she could sleep.

Imagine my surprise when she decided to go back to her home town for the weekend with the intention of visiting him. "For closure," she said. "I think it will help."

I told her I hoped it would work and preceded to give myself stomach ulcers, worrying they would get back together, or maybe she would be sliced up by him. Hell, maybe she would decide that she liked some *other* hometown friend I'd never heard of (a surprise ending! With a new character! All too likely!).

Sitting in front of my computer, I was barely able focus on the Mongol army I had to crush for my civilization to survive and flourish. The bastards took out some key border cities and my distraction led to my destruction by pony archer. Fuck you Genghis Khan, I don't need this shit right now.

The pitter-patter of hoofbeats from Khan's war-ponies over my capital city's formerly glorious town square made me even more certain something bad was going down with Rachel, and there was nothing I could do about it.

When Rachel got back, we drove around a bit and found an empty parking lot to chat/make out in, and she confirmed what I had dreaded right away. "I cheated with my ex while I was back home."

My jaw dropped, my eyes clouded over and I sat silently for what might have been a few days, but was probably just a few seconds. She said "Sorry, I didn't mean to. I didn't really want to. It just happened. Sorry."

To understand what happened next, you have to know a little bit about my approach to dating after a year or so of experience.

Most of what I knew about relationships came from books I had read, and so in my mind, it stood to reason if I did the same things the heroes in the books did, I had a pretty good chance of coming across as a good guy rather than the villain or the dolt.

Of course, most of the books I was reading at the time were fantasy novels, full of protagonists who were self-sacrificial on a mythical scale. Every story ended with them taking the full burden of every problem upon their shoulders and somehow saving everyone through their sacrifice. What would they do in this situation? I'm thinking they would say...

"It's okay, don't worry about it. I'm just glad you're safe. Don't get upset, I'm good. We're good." I wasn't good. I was destroyed. My self-confidence? Completely demolished. Fuck fuck fuck.

Things were never quite the same between us after that, though we stayed together for another eight months or so. I felt like we were going through the motions, acting the way we were supposed to act, but neither completely satisfied with the situation or with each other.

When Rachel broke up with me, I was kind of expecting it, and though I cried and was upset for a few hours, I quickly realized I was also free. Free from having to break up with her, which was something I thought would happen eventually, even though I questioned whether I could ever work up the courage to do so.

I had yet to come across a novel where the protagonist had broken up with the person he thought was his one, true love.

Laura

A week after the breakup with Rachel, I found myself in the back seat of my car with Laura, a relative newcomer to my group of friends, and probably the best-looking girl who had ever spoken to me. Picture Natalie Portman with short hair, unfairly large breasts and a funky sense of style and you've got a pretty good image of Laura. I was in heaven but confused as to how I had found myself there.

What happened was this:

Laura had dated a few of my friends, and was in my accelerated high school History and English classes.

She was just as awkward as I was, but in a different way. She was crippled by shyness, while I coped with my awkwardness by being extra loud and over-the-top. My assumption is she interpreted my clowning as confidence, and as a testament to the overwhelming power of confidence over the hearts and minds of some people, she started to come onto me. I hid my shock long enough to ask her out.

My friends *hated* Laura.

"She's going to be bad for you, Colin. You should just get back together with Rachel. What happened with you two?"

"I don't like that girl. I've heard that she gets around. I don't want her near me."

"You're invited to my birthday party, but I don't want her to come."

It should be noted these comments were all from my female friends, and my male friends had all either dated or wanted to date Laura, and had no criticisms on the issue.

That last comment about the birthday party struck a nerve with me, and in some kind of stupidly quixotic protest, I showed up to the party with Laura in tow. This resulted in the birthday girl starting to cry and her mother chasing us out. Laura was embarrassed, I was embarrassed, and my friends at the party were upset. This moment was an important one, as it represented the beginning of the end with that particular group of friends with whom I had been close for years.

Laura and I were a lot more sexually active than Rachel and I had been, and I got the impression Laura was convinced a lot of her value was derived from her appearance rather than her personality, so that's what she tended to flaunt and focus on.

At the time, this was perfect for me because it meant I had a highly sexualized relationship with a hot girl who wasn't a challenge to deal with or be around. Even the drama which inevitably popped up from time to time was easy to deal with, and we were always back on good terms shortly after an argument.

But eventually the drama did catch up with us, and no amount of sex or attraction could cover up the fact that we simply didn't get along very well, and we weren't going to be one of those couples that stayed together forever, or as it turned out, even a full year.

About eight months in, I broke it off, hoping we could stay friends but thinking she probably wouldn't be okay with that. I turned out to be very right. Not only would she not accept the breakup, but she also wouldn't accept we weren't going to have sex anymore.

Laura made a point of trying to seduce me the next chance she got, and things being as they were, she didn't have a terribly difficult time of it. I thought this would just happen once, or maybe for a week or two until we both got accustomed to being broken up. Several years later we were still hooking up, though, both a little co-dependent and unsure of how to be otherwise. The only thing that finally broke the ties was distance, and that only happened because I left for college in a city almost four hours away.

I learned a lot about myself and relationships from both Rachel and Laura. Those were formative years, and I'm a very different person for having dated both of them, though I'm not sure either of them realizes it.

Rachel broke me out of my shell and cracked open the protective barrier of denial I had built for myself. She also made me take some risks with my life I never thought I would be capable of taking. She taught me to kiss, and that intelligence is sexy. I also learned that being cheated on is not the end of the world, even if it seems like it at the time.

Laura introduced me to something I never thought a nerdy kid like me could have: physical confidence. Because of her I started working out, taking better care of my body, playing guitar, and wearing something other than Hawaiian shirts and cargo pants. Because of her I became more sexually competent and self-assured, and to this day her look and style is my 'type' when it comes to women.

Breakups suck, codependence blows, and drama is inevitable. But if you're able to learn something from every relationship, you can't help but come out a better person. I'm incredibly grateful for what I've learned from the women I've had the honor of dating, and I hope I was able to give back even half of what they gave to me, to them.

Tycoon Education,
Tycoon Opportunity

The Living Room Museum

In April of 2009, I was introduced to Henry Goldman.

One of the very first clients I picked up after starting my then-LA-based studio recommended me to Henry's personal assistant when she was asked for the names of talented UI (user interface) developers. This goes to show, by the way, there is an incredible amount of value in keeping relationships fresh; I still appreciate that old client, and make it a point to visit her business whenever I'm in town.

But back to Henry.

I was summoned to his massive West Hollywood penthouse/office with little idea of what to expect. I knew he had his hands in several different ventures, and he had made his fortune on Wall Street while working with one of the biggest players in the money-business a few decades before.

I dressed nicely, but felt distinctly under-dressed compared to the people walking into and out of the building at the address I was given. A few security guards eyed me suspiciously as they took the keys to my dated Honda CR-V to park it next to the shiny Mercedes and BMWs in the lot next door.

Instructed by the lady at the front desk who told me which elevator to use and which floor to get off at, I finally found the right door, knocked, and was greeted by Henry's personal assistant (the one who had found me), Greta.

Greta graciously asked me if I wanted anything to drink, something small to eat, or if she could get me anything else, and then launched into preparation-mode, reciting a list of rules and advice that sounded well-practiced.

Don't waste his time, but be sure to show personality. He respects that. Don't interrupt, but stand up for yourself. Don't, do, don't, do. I wasn't nervous before, but I was after that preparatory chat.

I sat down with a bottled water I hadn't asked for but which was brought anyway, and looked around the room in awe.

It wasn't a living room so much as a modern art museum. The walls were lined with propaganda posters (mostly from WWII, but also from WWI and other conflicts of the 20th century) and hanging or resting in every nook and cranny was artwork and industrial design pieces ranging from incredibly brilliant to terribly tacky.

The man was a collector, I could tell that already. This room was a testament to things he found beautiful; the successful bean-counter had become a curator, or at least a connoisseur.

Finally, 15 minutes after the scheduled meet-time, a large door opened on the far side of the room and three 20-somethings with computers and Wacom tablets clutched to their chests filed into the living room. One of the deepest voices I've ever heard called out some farewells, and then the voice's owner came to the door and invited me into his office.

Henry Goldman

First impressions are important, and the word that came to mind as I walked past Henry into his office was 'imposing.'

The guy had to be nearly seven feet tall, with broad shoulders, a barrel-like chest, and a massive frame to match. He wasn't a body-builder, but he was definitely not someone I would want to get into a shoving match with.

He had a bald head and bulldog jowls. His facial expression was serious, but with a hint of jovial happiness, as if he was having a good time being a little menacing. The look suited him.

To top it off, he was wearing what had to be at least 10-15 pounds of jewelry. Gold lion rings on several fingers, a big gold Star of David necklace encircling his neck, and a watch probably worth more than all of the money I'd earned in my entire life.

His office was full of beautiful, high-design drafting tables and computer monitors, with an entire wall covered in 30" screens, each displaying different bits of information about tradable assets.

We stopped in front of a computer on one of the tables and I began to reach for my laptop to show him my portfolio when he said, "No, I don't need to see any of your work. Greta wouldn't have invited you here to see me if you weren't good. What I need to know is if you can do the work I need you for."

With that, he flicked on the computer screen and pulled me into his world.

On an intellectual level, it was one of the most interesting projects I've ever been involved with. Because of an NDA I signed I can't discuss the specifics, but suffice to say, it involved money markets and required my skills with UI design.

In order to do the work, I needed to know more about how these particular markets operated, and Henry seemed thrilled to talk about his passion, describing in great detail how everything fit together, what traders did to manipulate each moving piece, and how money was made by the smart investor.

In just one hour, I had learned as much as most people would be lucky to learn in a whole semester of business school.

The project was fascinating and the guy in charge was such a colorful and intelligent character, I was game to take him on as a client for sure, and we hadn't even discussed my fee yet.

I must admit I grew a little bit worried as he told me about making money, assuming he would be a harsh negotiator, and the small bond that had grown in the hour since I arrived would disappear if I negotiated too hard. Thankfully, he left the negotiating up to Greta, and the conversation went like this:

"What's the most you've ever made per hour for a project like this?"

"Uh, well, I usually charge $100/hour, but for some more complex projects it's $150/hour."

"The *most* you've made *ever* for a project like this? *Ever*?"

I thought she was toying with me, and hoping to get me to lower my prices, but I held steady. "Yeah, $100-150/hour is the general range."

She looked a little disappointed, and I found out why a second later.

"Okay, that's what we'll pay you. Let's have you come back in tomorrow and meet with Henry so he can give you more details and introduce you around."

I realized too late she had been trying to get me to name a *higher* price! Guess I shouldn't have assumed she was trying to low-ball me.

I came in early the next day, and the next, and the next. The time was paid, so I didn't mind, but it was stressful

191

because I got the distinct impression it would only take one misstep to go from 'favorite freelancer' to 'former freelancer.'

Meeting the rest of his employees reinforced this speculation; each and every one seemed capable and hard-working, but also more than a little afraid he would come down on them like a hammer. They all had luxurious cars and high-end clothing and expensive meals every day, but he held the keys to the castle and could cut them off at any time.

That first week, when I wasn't at home designing UI elements for Henry, I was at his office, sometimes going over the work I had done, and sometimes just chatting with him about his businesses and life.

In addition to his money-market ventures, he was a big believer in sponsoring the arts, and he used his money to pay for a handful of artists to live and create, Medici-style. He also partook in creating art himself, and had his own rap album (*That explains the bling*, I thought).

But he seemed especially thrilled to teach me what he knew about money, and we would while away our meetings with him showing me his collection of gold bars (I'm not kidding) and currency from around the world. He would tell me about the origins of symbols that make up the economic system, and give me books he thought I should read to expand my knowledge of symbolism and exchange.

Tempting & Stressful

Eventually, he started hinting.

Little hints, nothing concrete, but he would drop small comments implying he might be interested in hiring me more full-time, if I was interested.

I artfully dodged each time, neither accepting nor declining the invitation, more like circumnavigating the question, expressing my gratitude for the thought. It was a bit strange, because even as he was making these pseudo-offers, I still felt I was walking on eggshells and just a step away from the whole thing falling apart.

Back home, I was stressed out.

Though I was living with my girlfriend, we rarely saw each other and when we did, my mind was so focused on Henry's project I wasn't very good company.

This was a huge opportunity though, and I didn't want to mess it up. I didn't know exactly where it was going, but the pay was great, I was learning a lot and I was getting one-on-one mentorship from a tycoon.

But it wasn't all sundaes and sunshine.

As I got to know Henry better, he would ask me to his office later at night to work/talk with him for hours and hours, in some cases causing me to miss plans I had with my girlfriend or friends across town. I also started to recognize that although he had a good time, he wasn't as happy as I had assumed.

One night he seemed particularly despondent and he confided he was interested in the massage therapist who came in to work on him several times a week. She was young and beautiful, and clearly made him happy, but I got the impression he knew deep down the relationship was just a professional one, and could only ever be professional.

Still, after telling me a bit about her and how long she's been coming to do sessions at his penthouse, he said "We haven't slept together or anything like that. I just like her a lot." His face spoke volumes about just how aware he was of the cultural and age differences dividing them.

There were also times I realized if I worked for the man on a regular basis, I wouldn't have the option of being myself.

At one point we were standing in his office and he was telling me about a project he was investing in, noting he wanted to build an Open Source version to allow more organic evolution to take place alongside the pro-upgrades he would also be sponsoring.

I thought it was a great idea and simply said *"Nice!"*

He turned his head and snapped "A person as intelligent as you shouldn't talk like an imbecile," and quickly moved on to another topic.

It all came to a head one day as I was about to leave Henry's office. He stopped me and said "Wait, there's someone I want you to meet."

A few minutes later, a good-looking, confident, suit-wearing man in his 30's strutted into the living room and greeted Henry.

I noticed a restrained bit of pride in Henry's eyes as he introduced us, then asked if I would wait in his office for a few minutes while they talked about private matters.

When Henry came back in the room, he said "I wanted you to meet him because he was my last *protégé*. He's running four of my businesses now and doing a great job at it. I'm very proud of him. He's made a lot of money for me and for himself, and you should see the car he just bought! In any case, he's capable of living his own life now, but I'm looking for a new *protégé* and I like the way you think about business and communication. I'd like to have you come work for me."

I had one of those moments, almost like during a breakup or being asked out by someone you've been secretly in love with, where something you thought might be coming but could never quite convince yourself was possible comes to fruition.

I think I held myself together outwardly, but inside I was thinking "Wait? What? Could I? Should I? How much would I make? What would I do? This could change my whole life!"

I calmly told him I was blown away by the offer, and that it was an honor just to be asked, but I would have to think about it. I told him I had already made plans to leave the country in a few months, and my ticket to Argentina was already purchased.

"But what will you do? What's your business plan while traveling?"

I recited a jumbled list of possibilities I had been going over in my head, including but not limited to running my branding studio from the road, starting up a video podcast for travelers, and making deals between vendors and sellers in different countries and acting as the intermediary. The ideas leaped off my tongue in rapid succession, and I could see that he was unimpressed, and wanted to tell me I sounded like a fool, but was holding back out of confusion or respect. Probably the former.

I was scheduled to see him again in the morning, and I told him I would take the night to think about it.

Sleeping On It

That night, I went back and forth over what I wanted to do and what I *would* do.

I wanted to leave LA because I felt overworked and stressed out. I didn't feel I was learning anything new, and I would be putting off my dream of traveling the world long-term once again if I took another geographically fixed position.

I had also promised myself I would never work for someone else ever again, knowing full well what happens to the good work I produce when put into the hands of a non-designer. On top of that, I'd never felt more stressed with a client than I did with Henry, so why would I subject myself to that on a daily basis? For the money? For the chance to be taught by one of the greats? Well, yeah. Those would pretty much be the main reasons to do it, actually.

I already knew Henry had more money than he could ever spend, and that he wasn't shy about dousing his employees in cash to get good work done round-the-clock.

He had taken a personal interest in me, and if I worked for him I'd likely get to take a golden escalator up the corporate ladder, with him figuring out where I fit best, while I got to learn all about how that type of business operates from the inside-out.

It was *huge* opportunity, but also a huge decision.

Down one path was success of the traditional kind: a good job, an impressive paycheck, integration into a network of the rich and famous, mentorship from someone who has been there and back several times, and has come out on top every step of the way.

Down the other path lay success of a different type, one that I couldn't quite put my finger on but which seemed very appealing: continuing to work for and answer to myself and only myself. Freedom of how I spend my time and where I spend it. Surrounding myself with the people I'm able to personally make contact with (but not being forced to spend time with people I *don't* want to be around). The ability to do exactly what I want with my life, so long as I'm smart enough to make it work.

I didn't sleep a wink.

Decisions, Decisions

The next morning I drove across town to West Hollywood, dropped off my car in front of the now-familiar building, and as I started to walk toward the lobby I heard Henry's voice from behind me call "Colin!"

As Henry walked toward me from about a block away, I realized I had never actually seen him out of his office. His imposing figure didn't look quite so imposing outside, and he was clearly making an effort to get exercise but having trouble due to some kind of mobility-related health problem.

I grinned and waved, and walking over to meet him halfway.

After exchanging hellos, we headed back toward his building and he asked "So what did you decide?"

I paused and then said "I have to go do this. I have to see if it's the right lifestyle for me or not, and what I can accomplish abroad. I need to get out of the country, if only for a little while."

Henry was quiet until we reached the automatic doors, which welcomed us into the lobby with a woosh of cold air. He said "You say you'll be there for four months, right?"

I said yes.

"Well in that case, when you're back in town, give me a call and we'll talk about the future. I want to be on your dance card when you're done with this adventure of yours."

With that, he headed inside.

I finished up the final bits of the UI project and emailed Henry the files, but didn't get a response from him, just one of his employees.

The final check I received from Henry allowed me to comfortably pay off the remainder of my college debt, and I set off for Buenos Aires a few weeks later, completely financially unencumbered.

I've been back in LA a few times since I started traveling, but I still haven't given Henry a call.

I think I'm afraid he won't remember me.

Chapter 8: Whatever the Weather

Thinking About Hallucinating

I've spent the last three days in bed, knocked flat by some kind of cold/flu/plague going around Reykjavík (which crawls its way from person to person throughout the city every year).

The seasons are changing in Iceland, and I can see it happening through the ginormous window that makes up one wall of my room. I'm sleeping about 16 hours each day, but only intermittently. Every time I wake up, the meteorological landscape has changed.

5am: it's drizzling.

8am: the wind is blowing the trees around like they're made of paper.

1pm: there are tiny chunks of ice falling from the sky like cluster bombs during wartime.

2pm: puffy, cartoonish snowflakes are drifting lazily toward the ground.

5pm: it's sunny, and people are outside playing with their children.

7pm: there's rain, and the wind is so strong the drops seem to be coming down horizontally.

10pm: somehow there's still sun on the horizon, but the atmospheric activity has subsided. For now.

I never really got sick until I started traveling.

Sure, I would have the occasional cold. I got food poisoning twice while in college (which I think speaks more to the quality of the food on campus than to my immune system's integrity). I picked up mono while in college, too, which is still a mystery to me since I wasn't kissing anyone at the time.

But new and interesting diseases have become par for the course when I arrive in a country, so much so that I expect within a month of arriving someplace unfamiliar I'll come down with *something*.

Usually it's small, whatever passes for the common cold in the area, and after giving myself a few days of cat-like slumber and relaxation, I'm back on my feet and no worse for wear.

Taking the time to relax is difficult though, especially when I feel like I'm wasting time, missing out on opportunities and hours in my day I could be using to do *anything* other than laying around in bed. Convincing myself that taking those days is actually a good investment is hard, but it makes sense if you do the math. The disease goes away much faster and I'm back in business. Few people even have to know I was out of commission.

There was one time in Thailand it didn't go so smoothly.

I woke up one morning with a monster headache and super-stiff joints. I was in my apartment in Bangkok, so I threw on some clothes and headed across the street to a massage studio that seemed reputable enough, and told the lady I wanted a neck and shoulder massage (for the uninitiated, this basically means they give you a Thai massage with a little more attention given to the neck and shoulder area).

I changed into the linen wrappings they provided and one of the women started to work on me. It felt good at first, but then I became acutely aware the air conditioning unit was right above me. Though it wasn't pointed in my direction, I started to feel very cold.

Not only that, but the massage therapist's hands on my skin sent ripples of pain through my body, as if every hair follicle had become an irritated nerve-ending, tweaked by her hands. I made it partway through the massage before making up an excuse to leave (I think I said I had a meeting I forgot about, but this is where things start to get a little fuzzy).

I changed back into my clothing and shambled toward my apartment, stopping on the way to get some water and painkillers from a 7-11, and some fried rice from a little place a few doors down from my building.

The first real indication something was wrong came when I realized I couldn't eat the fried rice.

The place I bought it from was one of my favorites—it cost less than $1 USD for a meal, and it was always delicious —but for some reason I spit out the first spoonful, and then trashed the whole meal. The smell was making me nauseous.

The extreme cold I had felt from the A/C at the massage parlor had increased, and even after turning off my A/C (sacrilege at that time of year in Thailand, it was so hot and humid) I was shivering, chills running up and down my arms, legs, and spine. Something was wrong.

Anything I touched—my chair, my bed, my clothing— sent lightning bolts of pain through my skin, like a full-body root canal, so I stripped off all of my clothing, downed a few painkillers and half a liter of water, and collapsed onto my bed, trying hard to ignore the pain, the chills, and the discomfort caused by my duvet and the sheets beneath me.

I woke up a few hours later in a puddle of sweat, though I wasn't sweating when I woke, which I assumed meant I had a fever. I tried to stand up but felt wobbly and light-headed, and I ended up crawling to the fridge in the living room and drinking more water, trying not to spill any, with only moderate success.

I crawled over to my computer and typed in my symptoms, hoping to figure out what I had. The first thing to pop up on the list was an ailment I had recently heard a whole lot about: Dengue Fever.

Shit.

I had heard of Dengue Fever before arriving in Thailand; I think it was one of the diseases you could die from in the old PC game *Amazon Trail*.

More recently, though, I had heard on the news it was a bad Dengue season in Thailand, and in Bangkok there had already been a handful of deaths, including a famous cyclist (whose death spurred the international news agencies to cover the disease and its prevalence).

Dengue, it turns out, is not something you can cure, and all the hospital can do is keep you hydrated and hope it doesn't turn into Hemorrhagic Dengue Fever, which causes you to start bleeding internally and can lead to a painful death.

I experienced a brief surge of adrenaline after reading that one of the most common reasons Dengue becomes Hemorrhagic is when an infected person takes painkillers. Or rather, the wrong type of painkillers. I shot up and wobbled my way over to the bathroom to see what kind I had taken earlier.

I collapsed to the floor in relief when I saw that I had, purely by chance, bought the one Dengue-approved painkiller they sold anywhere near me. I hadn't accidentally killed myself. Whew.

I drank more water, crawled back into bed, and the next two days went by in sped-up and slowed-down movie projection fashion. Everything was a little off-registration, colors seemed to blend together uncomfortably, and I hallucinated some very strange scenarios. My fever flashed in and out, though my only indication of this was waking up with my sheets drenched in sweat, but not sweating.

A full 72 hours later, I opened my eyes and the sun was shining through my blinds.

I thought 'Damn, it's hot' and turned on the A/C.

The air felt good as it started to fill my bedroom and I sat up straight, realizing my body didn't hurt anymore.

The sheets, though still damp, didn't irritate my skin. My brain seemed to be back in working order, and the last several days seemed like a dream. I took a moment to try to summon more than just snapshots and short clips from my memory, but already some of what happened during the past three days had become jumbled up with scenarios that were clearly dreams so that it was hard to separate fiction from reality.

I stood up, light-headed from not having eaten anything since I became sick, and despite the slight wobbliness I could tell I would be fine. I had made it. I wasn't going to die.

One more disease beaten. "And," I thought, "after that, anything else will seem like a fucking walk in the park."

I put on some clothes and left my apartment, looking forward to some fried rice.

Prepared to Disappoint

To some people, I'm a constant disappointment.

It's not that I am not achieving all they hoped I would achieve. I work hard, and there are few goals others have set for me I'm not reaching.

It's an issue of time and attention. Or more specifically *my* time and attention. It's the way I spend it that people are disappointed in, and sometimes this is more obvious than others.

Right now, I know my roommate Stig is disappointed in me because a few minutes ago, he came into my bedroom and insisted, through slurps of spaghetti, I come watch a movie with him. "It's amazing movie," he says in his Polish accent. "You should come watch with me and it will be fun."

But I'm busy. I'm answering emails from readers. I'm writing. When I'm done, I want to finish reading a book I've been glued to. Stuff to do, people to neglect. It's how I roll.

I guess that's maybe too strong a sentiment, but that's how other people make me feel sometimes.

After telling Stig I wasn't interested, but that I would definitely watch it at some point, he drooped a little and said "You're always busy. Always doing something. I'm loooonnnneeellly." I've learned when he exaggerates being hurt, it means he really is hurt and is trying to hide it. Many people seem to do this, actually.

I feel bad, but what am I supposed to do? Go spend my time doing something I'm not interested in because it will make someone else's night? Sacrifice my own happiness for his?

Of course, that's what you're supposed to do. That's what I've done most of my life, and still do sometimes. When I'm focused, though, and when I'm conscious of what I'm doing and saying, it's easier to say no to the well-meaning people who want my attention.

My family caught on to this pretty quickly. They still invite me to come watch TV with them when I'm back home, but they don't push the issue when I decline (I *hate* watching TV, and really, haven't they heard of the Internet?). They make it clear they want me around (something most people like to hear), but don't try to force their values on me (like thinking that being in the same room with other people while watching sitcoms is fun). Perfect.

Those who haven't known me as long sometimes take offense, though.

I can think of three ex-girlfriends who had serious issues with my need for alone time. They didn't understand why it stressed me out to have someone else around constantly, even when performing the most mundane and anti-social tasks.

What I considered to be personal time, they saw as a slap in the face. To them, it was the equivalent of me saying "I don't want you around," when in reality I was saying "I don't want anyone around."

It's time for myself I crave, and it can be incredibly difficult to find sometimes.

When I'm not able to spend enough time alone, I notice a huge difference in my mental state and intellectual performance. I don't make connections as quickly, I get stressed out more easily. I'm often tired.

I like people. People are great and inspirational to me. How people act, what they do. The people I choose to surround myself with are a big part of what keeps me motivated and enjoying life.

But not all the time.

Sometimes I need to be in my head. Sometimes I'm forced to disappoint someone because their values are not my values. Sometimes I unintentionally offend good people because I don't want to watch the evening news with them.

Is this my fault, or theirs?

I understand I'm in the minority with my predisposition toward periodic antisocial behavior.

From the day we're born, we're taught working together and community are the most important things in the world; that 'plays well with others' is just as, if not more, important than how intelligent, capable, or healthy you are. Some would say you actually aren't any of these things if you don't also play well with others.

I recently met a girl who was passing through Reykjavík on her way back to school after a vacation jaunt around Eurasia. After a few minutes of conversation over dinner, she and Stig decided what I do with my life, and the way I view social situations, is a symptom of some kind of disorder.

If I was healthy, they told me, I would be more like them, or at the very least I would *want* to be more like them, surrounding myself with other people at all times and feeling uncomfortable when alone.

It would have been rude to tell them that from my standpoint, theirs was the unhealthy lifestyle. To always need the company and approval of others to feel healthy? To need the attention of others to feel good about yourself? To seek reaffirmation from people whose values you may or may not share? Which is the stronger philosophy here, and which is just more common?

Of course, balance should be sought when possible, and I make every effort to split my time equally between other people and myself, but according to their argument, not being on the extreme far side of where I am is borderline psychotic. If I don't get uncomfortable being alone, then there's something wrong with me.

I sometimes wonder if I might have a bit of the social anxiety disorder my mother has. It's something she had to overcome after decades of health issues originating from the stress she felt being around people all the time. Might my own discomfort be something similar?

Maybe, maybe not. Either way, I still feel on a philosophical level one should not live their life for someone else. To do so is to not respect your own life very much, because if it's so easy to give away your time (which is the only truly finite resource you have), you must not feel like you'll do much with it otherwise.

To give your time away so easily can also negatively impact relationships, as it can mean giving value without necessarily receiving any in return.

It may seem a bit perverse to look at relationships as exchanges, but I feel the healthiest relationships are based on a balanced exchange of value. Both people give and receive about the same amount, even if the currency is different for each person.

If I gave up my night to go watch that movie with Stig, I would be giving value but not getting any in return, and over time I would grow to resent him as someone who is using me.

I'm often asked by self-improvement bloggers and their ilk how I'm able to get so much done in so little time. Focus your attention on balanced relationships instead of self-sacrifice, and you'll have less trouble getting around to the things you want to do.

It's not about being cold or hating people, it's about refusing to sacrifice *your* happiness for theirs. If everyone shared that same sentiment, no one would be looking for self-fulfillment by giving away something that, if retained, would help them become more fulfilled.

But the world doesn't work that way, so if you do decide to aim for happiness over self-immolating charity, be prepared to disappoint everyone but yourself.

Glorious
Unpredictability

A few days before starting my final semester of college, a massive cold front plowed its way through the Midwest, and Springfield, Missouri was blasted by what's called an ice storm.

For several days it had been raining. A lot. It rained and rained and rained so much that all of the trees were super-saturated with water, full to the brim and beyond.

Then one night the temperature dropped very quickly, and all that water inside of all those trees froze within a few minutes. If you remember anything from science class, you probably recall that as water turns to ice it expands, and that's what the water did to those trees.

BOOM. Almost every tree in Springfield exploded or shattered in a single night. The next morning, the whole city looked like a bomb had gone off.

The roads were unnavigable and completely covered in chunks of tree. Power lines were knocked down and pipes were frozen or destroyed, leaving thousands of homes without water and many more without *hot* water.

Gymnasiums and stadiums opened as shelters and the first day of the semester was pushed back two weeks to give crews a chance to clear the roads so students could safely make it to class.

My girlfriend at the time and I, along with a few friends, fled the city, driving slowly in a caravan of SUVs and off-road vehicles along ice-covered highways to the next town over which hadn't been hit as badly and still had electricity, water, and other necessities.

The drama of fleeing town and seeing all the destruction firsthand was wild, but that ice storm wasn't the worst natural disaster I've ever witnessed.

I was living in the Bay Area during the earthquake of 1989, and though I was only four years old at the time, it left an indelible impression on me.

Later, when I moved to Missouri at age 9, until I left for Los Angeles at 22, it seemed like every year brought new and interesting tantrums from the gods, and I grew to have a healthy respect for just how powerful nature can be. Tornadoes, floods, hailstorms, and lightning strikes became somewhat common, so when weather shocks or terrifies me these days, it has to be pretty spectacular.

Which brings me to today.

At this very moment, I'm looking out my bedroom window at the most intense wind storm I've ever seen.

It's been blasting my building all morning, which means after a night of partying and returning home at 7am, I'm unable to sleep away the alcohol because of the raucous pounding of the wind against my window. And the roof. And the whole world, as far as I can tell.

There's a small strip mall a block or so away, and the wind just shattered a window on that building. It didn't even hurl a projectile, the wind *is* the projectile. Like invisible fists from heaven.

But despite my wariness and understanding of how dangerous and powerful this kind of storm can be, I have a crazy fascination with it. Knowing the mechanics of wind, of rain, of sleet, and how—strong as the human body is—I could walk outside right now and be tossed around like a blade of grass. It's a heady, humbling feeling, and one I love to experience when possible.

Maybe this is just a rationalization, but I don't think the desire to have control taken away, especially if you're someone who is generally in control of most situations, is an uncommon one. It's nice to feel, even if just for a moment, whatever happens isn't your responsibility. If something bad happens it's not your fault, and there's nothing you could have done to stop it. Shit happens.

Of course if you take a step back and look at the bigger picture, this is completely untrue. You have the power to *not* put yourself in situations where you have no power.

I could choose to stay inside rather than going out to be buffeted by the wind and pummeled by tiny slivers of ice. Even so, in the moment it's wonderful to have nothing on your mind except how the world is impacting you, rather than the other way around. How it feels and what is, rather than how it could be and what you need to do to make it that way.

The world needs people with solutions. People who think they are right and who won't let gale-force winds, exploding trees, or other manifestations of an uncaring, flailing global weather system stand in their way.

But I'm still going outside. I'm going to release the reins of responsibility a bit, even if just for the span of a walk to the grocery store.

Because you know what? Sometimes the best way to keep control of your life is to loosen your hands on the reins.

Wee-Beasties

A teeny-tiny little insect just flew in my window.

Before the wee-beastie has a chance to do more than quickly peek around the room for traces of sugar or blood or whatever it happens to be craving, I smash it with a beanbag lying on my desk and sit back to analyze my response.

I chalk up my quick insect-killing reflexes to the time I spent in Thailand, where I was repeatedly traumatized by packs of vicious mosquitoes rampaging their way across the city every night, Hell's Angels-style, bloodying any poor American who was foolish enough to get in their way.

Unfortunately, they were *everywhere*, so there wasn't really any place to hide. I stayed in a fairly nice apartment while living in Bangkok, and despite never opening the windows and doing my best to clobber anything small and fluttery as soon as I saw it, I was still assaulted by mosquitoes every single night.

On top of the general discomfort resulting from being covered in tiny, itchy bites, I also caught a relatively mild (but still incredibly painful) case of Dengue Fever from some enterprising plague-spreader.

To be clear, I don't hate bugs. I'm not afraid of them, either. That's why I'm looking down at this splatter on my windowsill that used to be a fly or gnat of some sort and wondering if my reaction, my killer instinct, is permanent.

Are no creepy-crawlies safe around me? Should I be banned from any kindergarten with a pet tarantula? Should hissing-cockroach-owners ward me away with crucifixes and torches?

Probably not, but Iceland is an ideal place to break the bug-crushing habit in case it *has* become a part of my nature.

The response to bugs from most people here seems to be something along the lines of "Eww, yeah, I'm glad we don't have those." Locals say this with a full-body cringe, as if the idea of having bugs in your country is akin to having lice in your hair; it happens, but it's kind of your fault for not showering more often if it does.

This isn't an uncommon tendency, though, to look down on other countries for their peculiarities, and it extends far beyond what winged little monsters happen to be native to a given climate or region.

In the States, for example, we look down on any country that doesn't regulate the use of certain medications the way we do, and that don't have water you can drink straight from the faucet.

In Argentina, any country that doesn't have enough red meat for each person to eat a metric ton of each day is hardly worth calling a functional state.

Many people from New Zealand would be aghast to live in a place where there is any measurable amount of crime.

Every country has mosquitoes, even if their mosquitoes are not literal blood-sucking insects. Thankfully, there are positives in each country that make life there worth living, as well.

While I may whine about the bugs in Thailand, their food was a hell of a lot cheaper than it is in Reykjavík, and the general cost of living was about a million times lower.

Because I take so much away from each country I visit, I'm actually morbidly fascinated and a little bit concerned as to what kind of person I'll be a year or two from now, when I've had the chance to live in even more countries.

The mixture should prove to be a jumble of positives and negatives: true, I swat bugs like it's a hot new trend after living in Thailand, but I'm also a lot more aware of the difference between society's haves and have-nots, which is something I probably wouldn't have picked up in Iceland or New Zealand, where the homeless and impoverished populations are much smaller and less obvious.

Travel, for me, is about experiencing these contrasts—the inconsistencies within different societies—around the world.

If I know the pros and cons of different lifestyles, if I know what some cultures and governments and communities do right and what they do wrong, I'll be much more capable of discovering what I value and how I can help nudge things in a more positive direction wherever I happen to find myself.

There's an innate bias in everything we do. Our concepts of 'good' and 'bad' are subjective, and we, along with our ideas, are products of our culture and upbringing.

So the more information and perspective I have to work with, the better.

Bugs, and my newfound propensity for smashing them, may someday help me solve the problems I see in the world around me.

If you're not happy with the way things are but don't see anything to swat at, maybe it's time to step a bit out of your comfort zone and see what problems present themselves.

Then you can figure out how to smash them.

Freaker by the Speaker

My hand is on the speaker.

I'm pausing for a moment, taking a sip of my beer. Things escalated pretty quickly, as they tend to do.

The men dancing around me are businesspeople. A few still wear their ties and suits from a presentation they gave earlier, looking for venture capital and discussing various professional, adult things with other professional, adult people.

A tie flutters into my face and I set down my beer, removing my hand from the speaker to pivot and sway with one of the professional, adult men. He makes eye contact, shoots me a quick grin, and ungracefully wobble-dances back into the crowd.

I can't help but smile at the ridiculousness of it all as I put my hand back on the speaker, fingers seeking out the vibrations shaking the legs of my pants and making the floor beneath my feet shift seismically.

The overhead bulbs are off, but there is a colorful light show flashing spastically in time with the tempo of the music, and I thank my lucky stars I'm not epileptic. That would make Iceland a difficult place to live.

Or any place with a nightlife, really.

Where there is money, there are clubs and where there are clubs, there are flashing lights and businesspeople tribal dancing with hippies, and beer spilling on shoes but going unnoticed. My mind goes blank as I try to sync my pulse with the music coming through the speaker. It doesn't work.

I'm drunk. At least it's been vodka up until this point, so it should be a hangover-free morning. That's a good thing. A beautiful girl sashays by, glances at me from the corner of her eye and does a double-take before taking another step. She turns and walks right up to me, puts her hand on my left cheek and tip-toes up to plant a kiss on my right one.

She smiles, winks and walks off to join a male companion I didn't see before (drunken tunnel-vision?) who didn't seem at all disturbed about her tangent. You can't make this stuff up.

There are a goodly number of fashion-forward people in the club tonight. There was a fashion festival in downtown Reykjavík, and thousands of people from out of the country joined the style-aficionados from the Icelandic provinces in overrunning the city, causing the only traffic jam I've seen since arriving.

The crowd stuck around: this place is packed, and if I weren't standing back out of the way, hand on the speaker, back to the wall, I would be a little worried about catching an elbow in the face.

I experience a moment where time seems to slow down. You know the kind.

The music seems to pump from the speaker like jelly, thick and tangible. The businessmen frolicking wildly around me seem to be interpretive dancing, slowly carving out shapes in the air, losing themselves in the crowd. The colors all make sense together, the physical sensations I feel seem relaxing and fit perfectly with the general movement in the room.

It's a bit like meditation, where you're supposed to be at one with everything around you. I can taste the air being inhaled by the people around me, feel the stickiness of the floor through the shoes of the bartender rushing back and forth to fill orders I can remember placing and taking.

It's kind of like chaos theory, where each individual component has its own math, and now that I've seen the formula, gotten a sense of the big picture, I can see what's going to happen and know the reasons for what's happening now. Each motion has a cause and that cause has a cause and that cause was started by a motion I can also see.

I'm a watchmaker who has twisted the springs that turn the sprockets that move the arms that are flailing into my tunnel vision.

My shoes become propellers and my jacket is a flag and everything starts moving and flapping and twirling around like a dervish. My center of gravity falls out and I'm not sure if I'm about to fall or fly. My feet tap and the room taps with me. My eyes flash and the lights flash back.

I pull away into the crowd and my hand breaks contact with the speaker.

Reality slams back into place with a mental 'THWUMP-KA-THWANG,' concrete on metal on mind. I'm standing still and everyone around me is just drunk, dancing around like weirdos. There's beer on my shoes. Who spilled beer on my shoes?

I step back over to my drink, take a few sips and set it down half-full on a vacant table a few feet away. I gesture to my professional, business-people friends who are tearing up the dance floor, flash them a quick wave goodbye before dodging and excusing my way out the front door.

The air is cold. My hands are in my pockets.

I start tapping a rhythm on the inside of my jacket and my mind follows its lead.

I wait for things to escalate. And they will.

Acknowledgments

This was a very difficult book to write, partially because the stories I'm sharing are a bit more personal than what I generally discuss online, but also because the format required a slightly different style of storytelling than I've become accustomed to.

A preliminary thanks to my family. It's great to have you guys as a smiling, supportive safety net in the back of my mind, ready and willing to catch me just in case I take one risk too many and fall off a cliff somewhere. Thanks to my father and mother in particular, for raising me and other small details like that.

I'd like to thank everyone I've met these past few years while on the road. You quite literally made this book possible by being awesome and strange and memorable.

I'd also like to thank everyone I knew before I started traveling. Thanks for inspiring and teaching me what I needed to know in order to pursue my ideal lifestyle.

And finally, a special thanks to Molly Wright and Joshua Fields Millburn for helping me whip this book into shape. Molly (my mother) was gracious in tearing apart my wording at every turn, and then softening the blow by inserting smiley faces after every criticism. Josh (a very talented blogger and novelist) pushed and pushed and finally was able to bleed a little more expression from my words, though my storytelling still doesn't hold a candle to his.

And thank you for snagging a copy of this book. Let's be friends.

About the Author

Colin Wright is a person who is learning in public. He just turned 39.

He travels a fair bit, juggles all sorts of projects and interests, and is fortunate to live a life filled with challenges, small victories, and wonderful people.

Visit colin.io to learn more about his books, podcasts, speaking engagements, and other such things.

Printed in Dunstable, United Kingdom